The Guild of Students at the University of the West Indies, St Augustine, 1962–2012

The Guild *of* Students

AT THE UNIVERSITY OF THE WEST INDIES, ST AUGUSTINE, 1962–2012

Shane J. Pantin
and
Dexnell G.L. Peters

The University of the West Indies Press
Jamaica • Barbados • Trinidad and Tobago

The University of the West Indies Press
7A Gibraltar Hall Road   Mona
Kingston 7   Jamaica
www.uwipress.com

© 2013 by Shane J. Pantin and Dexnell G.L. Peters
All rights reserved. Published 2013

A catalogue record of this book is available
from the National Library of Jamaica.

ISBN: 978-976-640-412-3

Cover photograph: Student Union building at the University of the West Indies, St Augustine, circa 1960s. Courtesy of the West Indiana and Special Collections, Alma Jordan Library, University of the West Indies, St Augustine.

Cover and book design by Robert Harris.

Set in Adobe Garamond 11/14.5 x 27

Printed in the United States of America.

Contents

Foreword / *vii*

Message from the President of the Guild of Students / *ix*

Preface / *xi*

Acknowledgements / *xv*

Abbreviations / *xvii*

1. Continuity and Evolution, 1962–1968 / *1*

2. Two Steps from the Maelstrom, 1968–1973 / *19*

3. Redirecting Radical Consciousness, 1973–1980 / *37*

4. Societal Division Abounds, 1980–1989 / *48*

5. The Continued Growth of the Guild, 1990–1999 / *62*

6. Conflict and Development, 2000–2011 / *74*

Appendix 1 Timeline of the Guild of Students / *91*

Appendix 2 Past Presidents of the Guild of Students / *93*

Appendix 3 Student Numbers, University of the West Indies, St Augustine / *95*

Notes / *99*

Bibliography / *107*

Index / *111*

Foreword

In October 2010, the St Augustine campus of the University of the West Indies (UWI) celebrated its golden jubilee. Though its predecessor, the Imperial College of Tropical Agriculture (ICTA), had existed since 1922, it was in October 1960 that ICTA merged with the then University College of the West Indies (UCWI) to form its second campus at St Augustine, the UCWI having first admitted students at Mona, Jamaica, in 1948.

To mark the occasion, I researched and wrote a history of the St Augustine campus, from its origins as a sugar estate, then to its becoming a government farm, then the site of the ICTA, then the second campus of UCWI, and finally (from 1962), a campus of the UWI. My book, *From Imperial College to University of the West Indies*, sought to give a comprehensive history of the place and the institutions which were and are sited there.

The book failed in that aim in at least one respect: I said virtually nothing about the Guild of Students. I did mention its predecessor, ICTA's Amalgamated Clubs, and I noted almost in passing that though a Guild of Undergraduates had been established at Mona in 1951, it was not until 1962 that the Guild was formally constituted at St Augustine. I also wrote of the ICTA dining hall, built as the college's social centre in 1927–28 (there are photographs of it in the book mentioned, on page 20); its renaming as the Guild Hall after the ICTA/UCWI merger; its further informal renaming by students as Daaga Hall during the 1969–70 period; and its destruction by fire in 1980. (Today, the impressive Daaga Auditorium occupies the site.)

But other than these references, there is nothing specific in the book about the evolution and contribution of the Guild of Undergraduates (later renamed the Guild of Students). And this is a significant omission, considering the important role that the Guild has always played in campus life at St Augustine.

I was delighted, therefore, when I learned that two students of the Department of History had been asked to research and write the history of the Guild, to mark its own Golden Jubilee (1962–2012). Their book fills a major gap in the documented history of St Augustine. Well-researched, based on a range of published and unpublished materials, as well as oral history interviews, this book is a welcome addition to literature on the campus. It should be of interest to anyone who has studied or worked at the campus, as well as, more generally, to readers interested in the social history of Trinidad and Tobago (and indeed the Caribbean, since over the years many of the Guild leaders and members hailed from other West Indian territories).

I congratulate the Guild of Students, as well as Shane and Dexnell for conceiving, funding, researching and writing this book, which makes a valuable contribution to the ongoing process of documenting the history of our campus.

Bridget Brereton
Emerita Professor of History
The University of the West Indies, St Augustine

Note from the Guild President

In 2012, the University of the West Indies at St Augustine celebrated the golden anniversary of its student guild. These celebrations prematurely began in 2011, not as a yearlong preparation in anticipation of the historical milestone of the student body but as a mistake in gathering the history of the Guild. History is important. Many thanks to Shane J. Pantin and Dexnell G.L. Peters for archiving our history – this is just a beginning. To date, the Guild of Students, in spite of its noble mandate and the amazing political period of the 1970s, contends with the reputation of being a cradle for national politicians involved in corruption. However, this telling perception, legitimized by some presidents and councils during our chequered past, is an unfair assessment of a Guild that has facilitated national triumphs and achievements in spite of the constraints of holding student office and, in many cases, the real and unequal power dynamics at play in student and university administration negotiations and discourse.

The survival and increasing relevance of the Guild in the functioning of the organized student body and its duty to be the voice and lobby for its constituents is critical to the success of the mission of the University of the West Indies and the broader project of regionalism. Against this background, this book presents a rich history that can shed light on a significant part of the Caribbean's complex past and may point the way to a more creative future.

Amilcar Sanatan
President of the Guild of Students 2011–2012
The University of the West Indies, St Augustine

Preface

In 2012, the Guild of Students at the University of the West Indies (UWI), St Augustine, Trinidad and Tobago, celebrated its fiftieth anniversary, a milestone it shared with the national and regional community, as both Trinidad and Tobago and Jamaica celebrated their fiftieth year of independence. The desire to commission a publication marking fifty years of the Guild's history prompted the request made to two students of history, Dexnell G.L. Peters and Shane J. Pantin, by the Guild's president for the academic year 2011–12, Amilcar Sanatan. The work subsequently embarked on involved eight months of research and writing, drawing together a rather scattered but adequately rich history.

This volume represents one of the first efforts at the UWI to craft a history of the Guild of Students on one of its campuses. For this pioneering history, the authors sought to give a general picture of the main issues, personalities and events that took place at the St Augustine campus. Throughout its history, the Guild confronted many recurring problems, of which perhaps the two most important were its relationship with the administration of the university and students' general apathy towards extra-curricular activity. Noticeably, this text circumvents any controversial matters which, it was felt, might be inappropriate for such a publication at this time.

In conducting the research, the authors focused on documentary sources available at the Alma Jordan Library of UWI St Augustine and the student administration archives. These sources included publications by the Guild of Students, by other student clubs and societies, and by the university, as well as official reports and correspondence. Secondary sources included *From Imperial College to University of the West Indies: A History of the St Augustine Campus, Trinidad and Tobago* (2011), by Bridget Brereton, and *The University of the West Indies: A Quinquagenary Calendar, 1948–1998* (1998) by Douglas Hall. Combined, the documentary evidence presented a fair picture of the events of the fifty-year period from 1962 to 2012. Given the constraints of time and resources, the study was restricted to the documentary sources that were readily available to craft the narrative.

In 1962, the two student bodies at the St Augustine campus were the Guild of Undergraduates and the Guild of Graduates. The former represented students who were yet to graduate from the university, whereas the latter, currently renamed the Alumni Association, represented those who had graduated. There were other criteria for membership of these bodies, but the majority of their members were either undergraduates or graduates. In 1997, the title of the student body was changed to the Guild of Students to include the many postgraduate students. Throughout this work, the titles are used interchangeably: the Guild, the Guild of Undergraduates, the Guild of Students.

The Guild of Students proper comprises the entire body of registered students pursuing a course of study. The organization that represents their interests on the campus is the Guild council, whose administrative offices are currently located at the Student Activities Centre at St Augustine. During the student body's history, the Guild council, rather than the Guild, led many events, but as a body representing student interests it captured what might be considered the expression of the students. Certainly, there were those students or clubs and societies not aligned to the Guild council's goals or objectives, but it is difficult to determine the extent to which this was the case. However, given the size of the student body, just over ten thousand by the 1990s, the active members of the Guild were the ones who influenced policy.

A recurring motif throughout the Guild's history has been its uneasy relationship with the university administration. The latter can be divided into a few recognizable categories. The first are the senior administrators, such as the principal, deputy campus principal, security personnel, registrar, bursar and librarian. They constitute the decision-making personnel on campus who direct and instruct campus policy. Other administrative staff include administrative assistants, who are directed to follow the instructions of senior staff. Academic staff include lecturers and, perhaps, researchers, and though part of the administrative structure, they have been seen as either for or against the interests of students, depending on their stance on critical issues. Finally, there are non-academic workers, and these include maintenance personnel and other support employees who at times confronted the administrative decision makers over wages or working conditions. Throughout the text "the administration" is used to refer to those who make decisions that affect students. Those decisions have at times led to confrontation when students felt such decisions were not in their best interest. Campus authorities often perceived students as immature and irresponsible, which was reflected in their dealings with the Guild. Likewise, the Guild perceived the administration as authoritarian and reckless in its decisions regarding students. While important decisions created tensions, even resulting sometimes in physical confrontation, such conflict did not significantly hamper the growth and development of the student body or the university.

Chapters 1, 2 and 3, written and researched by Shane J. Pantin, explore the early period of the Guild's history until 1980. The first chapter documents the period from 1962 to 1968 and explores the developments in this era as one of continuity and evolution. Chapter 2 examines the period 1968 to 1973, which was one of activism and ideological engagement. Its prominent events and personalities are examined in the context of the national eruption of the Black Power movement of 1970. Geddes Granger was a transformative figure in this period, setting the stage for leaders to follow. Chapter 3 examines 1973 to 1980, a period of transition when activism was a lesser force on the campus, but was still strongly vocalized in student publications.

Chapters 4, 5 and 6, written and researched by Dexnell G.L. Peters, explore three decades of the Guild's history, the 1980s, the 1990s and the 2000s. During the 1980s, a heightening of ethnic confrontation was noticeable, perhaps as a result of the developments of the late 1960s and 1970s. Greater consciousness of cultural and ancestral heritage created a far more tense atmosphere than in previous years. The period saw a return to fundamental practices which the Guild had followed in the early 1960s.

The 1990s was a period of development as the Guild expanded its facilities and created greater linkages with the student body. The Jamaat al Muslimeen insurrection of 1990, ironically, did not have as great an impact on the campus as might be expected. Instead, the Guild had a much more definitive role in the lives of students by becoming a facilitator and champion of their interests. This was seen in the expansion of the services it provided to the students in addition to the number of student activities planned.

Finally, chapter 6 explores developments over the last eleven years which saw the establishment of the Student Activity Centre, where the offices of the Guild of Students are currently housed. Previously, their accommodations were limited, having shifted from the old facility where Daaga Auditorium currently stands to the small confines currently holding the Disabilities Unit. The new space has facilitated greater participation by a section of students in the Guild's affairs, for not all students participate in the Guild's activities, as well as enabling it to have an established presence on the campus. This period also saw significant developments in constitutional reform, with 2008 being the definitive year of change. Long a recurring issue, then president Hillan Morean was able to chart a new constitution during this crucial period.

It is hoped that this history provides a brief glimpse of key developments and personalities that will generate further study of the Guild of Students which in turn might shed light on issues not mentioned in this book. In looking back, there were areas the authors did not delve into simply for a lack of space and time. But one of the goals of the publication is to make the student body as well as administrators and academics of UWI aware of the transformative events that shaped the St Augustine campus. If such is this publication's impact, then this history would have served a useful purpose in providing a resource for the engagement of the university community.

Shane J. Pantin
Dexnell G.L. Peters

Acknowledgements

We wish to acknowledge and thank those persons who made this project a reality. First, we must express our gratitude to Amilcar Sanatan, 2011–12 Guild president, who saw the importance of a history of the Guild and sanctioned the project. He was also involved in planning discussions and charting the course for the project. Claudia De Four, deputy librarian of the Alma Jordan Library, provided important advice and made the Main Library's resources and university's archives available for research, for which we are deeply grateful. We also acquired sources from the West Indiana division of the library and our requests for access to large quantities of student publications and storage space were readily facilitated. We must personally thank Kathleen Helenese-Paul and Lorraine Nero of this division.

Jo-Ann Georges, assistant registrar, campus records manager in the UWI Department of Archives and Records Management, was instrumental in our researching and collecting data from important sources, and she unhesitatingly accommodated the requests we made of her department. Karina Atisha-Ali and Ornella Thomas, our two student assistants, took up the gargantuan task of copying the countless records found in the library and the UWI archives. We are extremely thankful for the excellent and speedy job that they did. We also thank the administrators at the Office of the Guild of Students, including Satya Rambaran and Giselle Gobin-Chance, who were particularly helpful throughout the entire course of this project. The project spanned the terms of two Guild executives, and so we are grateful to the 2012–13 Guild council for its continuity. For this, we personally thank Kevin Ramsewak, president of the Guild of Students, and Mervin Agiste, public relations officer.

We must also especially thank Professor Bridget Brereton, who willingly, warmly and efficiently gave us advice, critiqued, proofread and corrected numerous drafts of the manuscript. Professor Rhoda Reddock, deputy principal of the St Augustine campus, made invaluable contributions in the final stage of the project and is most appreciated.

Finally, we wish to thank you, the readers, for your interest, and hope that you find this monograph a rich and insightful history of a major institution of the University of the West Indies at St Augustine.

Abbreviations

EAC	External Affairs Commission
ICC	Inter-Campus Committee
ICTA	Imperial College of Tropical Agriculture
IUS	International Union of Students
JFK	Auditorium John F. Kennedy Auditorium
PNM	People's National Movement
SPIC	Society for the Promotion of Indian Culture
STAN	*St Augustine News*
UCWI	University College of the West Indies
UWI	The University of the West Indies
WIGUT	West Indies Group of University Teachers

Chapter 1

Continuity and Evolution, 1962–1968

In 1962, the Guild of Undergraduates of the University of the West Indies (UWI) at St Augustine, Trinidad, was endorsed via the Royal Charter given to UWI when it became independent of the University of London. The objectives of the Guild upon its endorsement, as articulated in its constitution, were simple: "the furtherance of educational and social purposes of the undergraduate student body of the University of the West Indies, the furtherance of its common interest, as well as the advancement and promotion of unity and fraternity among the members of the Guild". These were the same objectives followed by the Guild of Undergraduates of the predecessor University College of the West Indies (UCWI). The pursuit of these objectives was coordinated through Guild committees, which were smaller bodies assigned particular functions. Continuity and evolution best describe this transition. Continuity refers to the concerns of the Guild prior to the emergence of UWI's St Augustine campus which remained concerns in the period thereafter. Evolution refers to the challenges and changes confronting the Guild in this period which tested its ability to be an effective voice of the student body. The result was a mix of old and new, tradition and dynamism, which for a time coexisted somewhat harmoniously.

Formalization

Contextually, the Guild's history is linked to the three-stage development of the St Augustine campus. The first incarnation was the Imperial College of Tropical Agriculture (ICTA), a science-based tertiary-level institution devoted to training in and research on tropical agriculture. In 1960, following ongoing discussions between regional leaders, ICTA was absorbed into the Jamaica-based UCWI. The site at St Augustine was transformed, introducing the Faculty of Agriculture and the Faculty of Engineering, which augmented student enrolment. In 1962, the university once again changed status, becoming the University of the West Indies formalized by Royal Charter. Previously, all degrees awarded to graduating candidates were from the University of London. Now the university had the authority to award its own degrees to students as graduates of the UWI.

In all three incarnations, there were bodies representing student interests. The campus at Mona, Jamaica, had its own Guild of Undergraduates. The ICTA had various student clubs and societies which Bridget Brereton notes were known as the "Amalgamated Clubs".[1] Many of these clubs catered to sporting tastes, including the Rugby Football Club, Association Football Club, Hockey Club, Tennis Club, Rifle Shooting Club, Golf Club and Indoor Games Club (that included table-tennis, billiards, bridge). There were also clubs that catered to other tastes such as the Art Group, Music Group, Culture Club, Camera Club and Natural History Society.[2] Some clubs fared better than others, with the Rugby Club appearing to be well supported but the Hockey Club going through travails in membership, as stated by one of its representatives, J.M. Suttie: "Hockey at the College is in a sad state this season."[3]

With the formation of UCWI, the charter established two bodies: a Guild of Undergraduates and a Guild of Graduates. All matriculated students (that is, all students who were registered with the college and were following a course of study) were members of the Guild of Undergraduates. The Guild of Graduates represented alumni, and anyone who received a degree from the University College could then apply to become a member of the Guild of Graduates.

The Guild of Undergraduates continued its work following the ratification of UWI. The constitution of the UCWI's Guild was simply adopted for the

UWI's Guild and the concerns of the "new" Guild remained the same. Some of these concerns included the perception that the administration was not paying attention to the demands of students and that the student body was not contributing sufficiently to the life of the university. In the 1962 issue of *Sundowner*, the annual magazine of the UWI St Augustine campus which had been inherited from ICTA, an article opined, "Relationships between administrative staff and students tend to be rather strained. It is hoped that both sides will endeavour to create more concrete links so that better understanding and wholehearted cooperation can grow out of full knowledge of each other's activities."[4] Regarding students, it stated, "Problems that confronted the Council were many and varied. The attitude of many of the students to extra-curricular activities left much to be desired."[5] Apathy was a continuous concern for the Guild, with an editorial in the 1966 issue of the *Augustinian* commenting bluntly, "Enough has been said about their lethargy. . . . We should like here to mention one important aspect of their lives: extra-curricular activities. A large number of them have none, save dances."[6]

At the same time, the university was evolving to meet external and internal challenges. In the 1960s, major increases in the number of students at UWI St Augustine tested the resources and capacity of the Guild to manage the demands of students and the administration. Likewise, the Guild also challenged the student body to think and act beyond narrow self-interest.

From 1962 to 1968, the Guild council endeavoured to become an important part of the lives of students by adequately representing their interests. It attempted to create regional and international links, educate the student body, create outlets for student expression, and contribute to the students' life on campus. In addition, the Guild had the challenge of maintaining harmony between the student body and administration, creating a congenial relationship between the student body and the Guild, responding to national circumstances, and working towards reforming the constitution of the Guild to reflect contemporary circumstances. The preliminary conclusion is that achievements in this period were fair compared with those of other periods, but importantly, the Guild managed to become an important centre for student concerns.

Continuity

The First Guild Council of UWI St Augustine

At the time of UWI's formalization, the Guild council consisted of fifteen members. This council, led by Hilbertus A.D. Chesney, was elected in June 1962 (as Guild council of UCWI St Augustine) – two months prior to the formalization of UWI – and served until 1963. A council for UWI was elected in mid-1963 with Percy DeGannes becoming the first president of the Guild of Undergraduates at UWI St Augustine; DeGannes was an engineering student from Grenada who graduated in 1964. Many of the officers of this first Guild were from other Caribbean territories, which reflected the spirit of the university in the years immediately following its ratification. It was an understandable development as regional students usually stayed on campus halls (dormitories), allowing them to be closer to the activities of the campus community.

The Guild operated at the Guild Hall (the former ICTA dining hall), with different amenities for activities. The *Fresher's Guide* for 1967 described the amenities and rights of access:

> Students are free to use the Guild Hall at any time during the day or night. It is their Common Room.
>
> Downstairs, there is a Cafeteria which supplies lunches and snacks at reasonable prices; a well-stocked air-conditioned bar with taped music; a photographic room and a VIP lounge. Upstairs, there is the Guild Office, the Publications room, the Billiards room, Music room and Television, [*sic*] Magazines, daily papers and current periodicals are also available. In the Annex of the Guild Hall are facilities for table-tennis and weight-lifting.[7]

The hall served two functions: housing the offices of the Guild of Undergraduates and as a primary centre for student activity. Albeit a small facility, it met the needs of the students at that time. But as student numbers grew, expansion of the Guild Hall was an area of concern for succeeding councils, which led to breakdowns in the relationship between the Guild and the administration.

Table 1. The First Elected Guild Council of UWI St Augustine

Name	Executive Position	Faculty Originating	Territory
Dominique Norman Percival DeGannes	President	Engineering	Grenada
Reginald Alfred Burgess	Vice-president	Agriculture	Jamaica
Oliver Stanley Brooks	Secretary	Engineering	Jamaica
Karl Wellington	Treasurer	Agriculture	Unknown
Noel Ivor Fernandes	Guild Hall secretary	Engineering	Guyana
Kenneth George Hoo	Guild Hall treasurer	Engineering	Jamaica
Weygand Fitz David Younge	External Affairs Committee chairman	Engineering	Guyana
Desmond Arthur Lee-Own	Inter Campus Committee chairman	Agriculture	Guyana
Ronald Lindsay Bartolo	Games Committee chairman	Engineering	Trinidad & Tobago
Franklyn Valantine Peter Harvey	Publications Committee chairman	Engineering	Grenada
George Winston Cole Maynard	Day students' representative	Liberal Arts	Trinidad & Tobago
Dennis George Robertson	Evening students' representative	Liberal Arts	Trinidad & Tobago
Carlyle Bonstan Albert Ross	Ex-officio member		Guyana

The Concern over Student Apathy

One of the common complaints by the Guild council, as well as those outside the university, was of the general apathy of the student body. The editorial in the 1962 issue of *Sundowner* stated: "It is felt that it might be advisable to point out that a university is not an institution in which one works three or four years solely for a degree. Nor will that degree be a passport for an easy life. Qualifications are little more than a 'quick to read' label of a man's ability, used when there is little else by which to judge him."[8] The importance of student participation in the development of the university as well as society was constantly stressed. The demands placed upon students stemmed from a particular view of education, especially tertiary-level education, and its contribution to society. The prevailing assumption was that persons entering tertiary-level institutions were future leaders, and this influenced the perception that a student's time at the university was inextricably linked to social and university obligations. Tertiary-level education for most people in the English-speaking Caribbean in the early 1960s was still an impressive achievement and the fledgling social and political institutions of Trinidad and Tobago made the university an elite and privileged institution. Its young members were expected to fulfil reciprocal social obligations in return for the opportunities granted to them. Given the frequent complaints, it seems these expectations were not met.

As a result, student participation in constructive activities at the university was repeatedly stressed. In 1963, for example, during the rapid expansion of the campus, the editorial in the *Sundowner* once again raised its concern:

> Are we, as students, joining in this exciting surge of planning, experimenting and building with the same foresight, sincerity and purpose?
>
> Student numbers must be expected to increase rapidly over the next few years and this will put severe strains on the yet recent organisation of the Guild. After all, extra-curricular activities are as important a part of University life as academic studies.
>
> Social functions are valuable in getting members together and creating that intangible Guild spirit, which can only form painstakingly. It is heartening to note that cultural activities are expanding but there is still tremendous scope for clubs to stimulate interest in music, art and current affairs by bringing speakers and films to the campus and holding debates.[9]

The 1964 *Sundowner*, in its editorial pages, suggested that students could be the agents of change, pointing to the example of the civil rights protest, the Greensboro sit-ins in the United States in February 1960, where four African American students defied racial segregation and sat in a restaurant to be served. It pointed to the responsibility of students and to the number of different avenues through which they could participate. Still, the editorial reached the conclusion that

> the majority of students are not willing to accept responsibility. They tend to shy away from anything taxing on the mind during their spare time, and prefer to indulge in the popular "S.T." or discussion on everything in which everyone says nothing. Of course, you can have an "S.T.", but accept some kind of responsibility, participate in the administration of your own affairs. If we do not run our own affairs, if we do not organize our own functions, if we do not think of new ideas to apply to our own Campus society, who will we get to do it?[10]

Sundowner was not the only publication to express concerns about students' lack of participation. *Magnet*, a publication by the Guild begun in the late 1960s, also highlighted this concern. Guild president Wilfred Phillips, in an address to the students, stated:

> Next comes the question of your participation in extra-curricular activities, more specifically, your attendance at public lectures. Attendance at lunch-time "teach-ins" and open lectures have been disappointing to us and discouraging to the speakers whom we invite. I recently received a letter from the Pro-Vice Chancellor in which he commented on the poor attendance at the recently concluded Open Lecture Series and in which he asked me to urge attendance at these quite informative series.[11]

Then, in a *Magnet* editorial a few months later, "We do not wish to imply anything obscene, but if [the students] were not working I wonder what they were doing. Poor attendance at meetings, failing societies, and an absence of political activity state that most were not helping the campus. Some of you were sleeping too much; some of you were gossiping too much; and some of you were playing too many games of all fours."[12]

The *Canadian*, a newsletter produced by students of the dormitory named Canada Hall, published an article in the first issue eye-catchingly titled "Student Interest in World Affairs", which stated that the students on Campus have displayed a conspicuous lack of interest in the burning issues that face mankind in the World today. This present state of affairs at an institute of higher learning where future leaders of the Caribbean would emanate, leaves one only to wonder what would be the content and discipline of the future West Indian Leaders who will be in authority to formulate economic, social and political policies, to steer our states from economic stagnation, repression and oppression.[13]

Another Guild publication, the *Augustinian*, printed an article titled "The Role of the Student in Social and Economic Development", which urged students to "participate in economic and social development on two levels: theory and action. Because of their status as an elite of young professionals, students should be free to analyse and suggest alternatives to the basic theoretical assumptions underlying the development plans of their government."[14]

Given the high expectations by wider society and the resources provided for expanding tertiary-level education, the Guild saw participation as important. Participation made the initiatives it undertook relevant and gave strength to requests made to the university authorities. But student apathy was not an easy issue to solve and this apathy has continued to the present. Those who chose to become conspicuously active participants in social and university issues did so as a vociferous but small movement. As witnessed in the years after 1968, student action as part of a radical movement unleashed an adverse response from those who expected student engagement to make more conventional contributions. The latter believed education should work with the established order to create a better society and not be a counter-establishment force wanting to establish its own ideas.

Publications

There were several publications produced by the Guild and other student groups in the early 1960s. Many were short-lived, giving glimpses of issues relevant to the students. These publications provide an important window onto the Guild's early history and are a valuable resource in creating a coherent history of the Guild. *Sundowner* was an annual magazine produced by the St Augustine campus. It was a diverse publication highlighting developments at the university and student activities. The magazine began under the ICTA and was published during the late 1950s to early 1960s with contributions from academic staff as well as students. The Guild used this publication for brief reports, at times supplemented with a message from the president. The diversity of the topics it covered shows the broad scope of development of the university at the time. However, its editorial policy was that of portraying a positive image of the university and attracting prospective students.

The *Guild Bulletin* was a newsletter that began around the mid-1960s and published Guild news and events. It was one of the few ways to circulate important information to students and each issue averaged no more than half a dozen pages, though it provided invaluable information on the work of the Guild and other events and activities.

The *Augustinian* was another diverse publication catering to students' tastes and included short stories, pieces about contemporary issues, as well as messages from various quarters. Its motto was "Expression leads to discussion". In referring to the Augustinian as both someone attending the university and the publication, the editorial commented that "the Augustinian is the voice on campus. And a loud one at that! He attempts to give stimulus to the world of ideas. He elicits discussion from all quarters in and out of the University. He awakens the lethargic and may step on a few corns. But he is neither conservative nor profane."[15]

Opinion was a student publication that began in 1961. As one of the earliest publications by the students at St Augustine, *Opinion* presented a wide range of items such as poetry, articles on the concerns of students in other universities and events on campus. An editorial discussing its origins explained that it wanted "to lay the foundation for student unity and expression".[16]

Magnet was a campus weekly newsletter produced by the Guild in the mid- to late 1960s. It notified students of news and events and was a forum for students to put forward opinions. Like the *Guild Bulletin*, each issue was about half a dozen pages, but this was one of the more opinionated publications in circulation. The *Canadian* was produced by students in Canada Hall in the late 1960s and early 1970s. Unlike other campus publications, the *Canadian* was well-funded and carried highly opinionated articles. It explored issues ranging from the economic regional integration project known as the Caribbean Free Trade Area in the late 1960s to the issues surrounding political activist (and UWI graduate) Walter Rodney, as well as the contributions of the students.

The common thread of student publications in the early 1960s was the broad range of topics highlighted; only a few catered to specific tastes. This range reflects the things students might have been interested in learning about. Poetry was a defining feature, with most of the publications carrying a poem in at least one of their editions. International events were another noticeable feature, particularly regarding information about the experience of foreign students and foreign universities. Finally, the campus community was another important focus, especially the university administration and its response to requests by the Guild. Overall, it is difficult to gauge the success of these publications in uniting the student community. If their short lifespan is any indication, then publications were perhaps a way for an enthusiastic group of students to briefly come together and produce a serial. Therefore, a single publication may not have had much of an impact, but the range of publications was indicative of student interests and perhaps a predictor of what their direction in the future would be.

Constitutional Reform

Constitutional reform was an important concern for the Guild during this period. First, the constitution in use was that of the old UCWI and did not reflect the transition to the UWI. Second, the constitution at St Augustine was patterned after Mona's student guild, and the succeeding councils after 1962 felt that the constitution should reflect developments at St Augustine. Third, since the transition to the UWI, there was a feeling that the constitution and administrative authority of the guilds on all three campuses should be harmonized. The last point was open to debate with concerns being voiced by successive councils in Trinidad and Tobago.

The effort to reform the constitution began as early as 1961. Some proposed changes included clarifying the wording of the constitution to reflect developments from ICTA to UCWI. One major change was that the Guild would from then on be referred to as the Guild of Undergraduates rather than the Students' Guild. Discussions on constitutional reform continued when Percy DeGannes assumed office, and he proposed a major reform: centralization of the guilds of the three campuses. Representatives from all three campuses were to convene and discuss this proposal.

Statute 28 of the university charter referred to the Student's Society, while ordinance 1 referred to the Guild of Undergraduates. In March 1964, F.H. Bowen, dean of students based at Mona, interpreted this to mean one student body for all three campuses with administrative branches at each campus. Prior to Bowen's interpretation, DeGannes had felt that such an interpretation was an accurate reflection of the charter and the Guild should proceed in that direction. In early December 1962, the constitutional committee of DeGannes (chairman), O.S. Brooks (secretary), A. Williams and F. Harvey met to explore the structure of a possible central executive of the Guild that would preside over all campuses. The committee discussed and proposed the composition of the central executive, methods of election, powers of the central executive, financing and the location of the Guild's headquarters, among other things. It is unclear whether this committee was to have presented its recommendations to the proposed meeting of guild representatives of the three campuses to be held later on.

The meeting of the three campus guilds was scheduled for the Christmas vacation 1963, but difficulties pushed the meeting to 19–24 February 1964. However, the representatives from St Augustine chosen to attend the meeting could not make the trip as a result of conflicting academic schedules. In addition, F.H. Bowen, in a letter to the secretary of UWI St Augustine, Victor Archer, explained, "It would seem that there has been a breakdown in the proper functioning of the Guild here (Mona), and Senate has appointed a Committee to look into the matter."[17]

In late 1964, a new meeting was arranged and part of the discussions there concerned the establishment of a centralized executive authority. The St Augustine Guild council for 1964–65, with Delf O. King as president, was not in favour of a guild with a strong central executive representing students throughout the university, because of existing problems. From 18 to 23 December 1964, representatives from all three campuses met to discuss the way forward. Due to that meeting, the St Augustine contingent agreed to a few changes, one of which was with regard to the length of the guild's term in office. A proposed set of amendments to the constitution was also drafted which referred to the establishment of duties and procedures of a central committee of the guilds.

It was agreed that each campus would vote on the proposed amendments and, if approved, they would be referred to the university's senate. However, St Augustine's president, Delf O. King, was under the impression that Mona and Bridgetown (before the campus was established at Cave Hill) had agreed to the changes and therefore sent a letter with the proposed amendments to the university's vice chancellor. But Arthur E. Burt, senior assistant registrar, in responding to this letter, stated that Mona and Bridgetown had sent no notifications regarding the changes, and this should be done first rather than St Augustine acting on its own. King responded to the senior assistant registrar with a letter, which Carl E. Jackman, secretary of UWI, described as "badly written, and borders on the verge of rudeness".[18] King's letter described the slow pace of developments at Mona and Bridgetown and said that St Augustine was prepared to act on its own regarding specific portions of the constitutional amendments.[19]

This letter greatly discomfited Burt, Archer and Jackman, for they could not understand King's impatience and felt that it was unbecoming to allow St Augustine to act on its own with regard to constitutional change without word from the other two campuses. A separate examination of the constitution of Mona's guild was made and its findings were approved by the senate. But any constitution with regard to all three campuses or to the individual campuses was still being considered. Be that as it may, as late as May 1965, Jackman alerted King that elections could go ahead at St Augustine in the absence of a constitution.

By August 1967, the question of the Guild's constitution was still being considered. Assistant registrar at St Augustine Austin Clarke, in referring to the matter, made the assumption that the Guild at St Augustine was operating under constitutional arrangements agreed upon in 1965. But acting registrar Eric L. Fraser stated that this was not the case and, in fact, the Guild was still operating under the old constitution of 1957, which was amended in parts in 1958. By early 1968, not much had changed. Despite a decade of ideas and discussions about reforming the Guild, no substantive gains had been made.

Evolution

The period 1962 to 1968 was one of expansion for the university. The number of students entering the university (see appendix 3) underlined the scale of this expansion. In 1963, the College of Arts and Sciences was established and a large influx of students from Trinidad and Tobago opted to do arts and science degrees. Whereas in 1961 and 1962, there were fewer than two hundred students, by 1966 there was approximately a 90 per cent increase in enrolment, which had an impact on the Guild's and university's ability to facilitate new recruits. A 1968 report on the university generally indicated that "for the existing student population, the resources available for scholarships, bursaries and loans are barely able to provide the number needing support".[20]

While exact demographic figures are not available, a fair guess about the student make-up in the early 1960s is that most were male and from relatively well-to-do backgrounds. As numbers expanded there was a greater female presence, especially in the arts. The programmes offered were diverse. There were programmes for evening students that catered to those who worked and were perhaps over the age of thirty and programmes for full-time students who might have come from a younger age bracket. In keeping with the vision of the ruling party of Trinidad and Tobago, led by Prime Minister Eric Williams, the goal was to train and develop a cadre of teachers, administrators and technicians capable of developing national society:[21] students entered the university not solely to pursue academics but to become certified in a particular field. By 1968–69, with over one thousand students, the Guild had to keep pace with these developments which created different challenges. Efforts were made to expand facilities with some success.

One important characteristic was that many students entered science-based programmes. The two commanding faculties, agriculture and engineering, attracted a sizable number of regional and local students. But rigorous expansion introduced programmes in the humanities and social sciences as well. The range of subjects the university offered included physics, chemistry, zoology, botany, mathematics, English, French, history, sociology, government (political studies), economics and management. Bridget Brereton noted that "hundreds were registering . . . in numbers St Augustine had never seen".[22]

Forming Regional and International Links

The Guild established regional and international links with other tertiary institutions, international organizations and government agencies, which was an important development in the light of the failure of the British West Indies federation (1958–62). This failed effort at Caribbean integration did not dampen the enthusiasm of students to connect with regional peers. A committee of the Guild, the External Affairs Commission (EAC), reported on a successful mission its members undertook to Grenada in early 1966, and urged for a greater push "to woo the Islands to sending more students to the UWI"[23] by sending similar missions to St Vincent, St Lucia, Dominica and Antigua.

Internationally, the Guild attempted to create opportunities for future students. One example of this was a meeting with the US ambassador by Guild council members in April 1966, at which a number of concerns were addressed, including the desire to establish greater links between the US embassy and the Guild. One concern was a programme of scholarships to Latin America arranged by the American government which did not include the Commonwealth Caribbean. The exclusion of the English-speaking region was one point they sought to address. The Guild also sought the US embassy's assistance in achieving some of its goals. Anthony Gonzales, president of the Guild, concluded that the meeting "made an important break-through in its effort to establish international contacts, and to make this young institution of ours receive the pulse of the outside world".[24]

This spirit of international engagement continued with the attendance of Anthony Gonzales and E. Henry Sealy, EAC chairman, at the International Student Conference, held in Nairobi, Kenya, in August 1966. At the time, these conferences organized workshops, seminars, panel discussions and international tours for student unions throughout the world on social, economic, political and environmental topics affecting the global community. The conference also allowed them to view the workings of student unions in France, England, Scotland, Canada and the United States.

Finally, through its publications, the Guild provided articles on important regional and international events. Some of these related to social issues affecting a foreign country, such as civil rights in the United States or the activities of student unions in Europe. The region was also highlighted in reports on politics or an upcoming annual festival in a regional territory.

It is unclear what impact the initiative to establish international and regional links had. It did allow the Guild council members to undertake trips to foreign countries and connect with groups and organizations. But in the short to medium term there were no decisive outcomes from these initiatives as it was difficult to distinguish between the initiatives of the Guild and those of the university. This may, perhaps, indicate the harmonious alignment of the Guild's and the university's policy regarding certain activities in this period.

Expression and Communication

Students had interesting ways in which they expressed and communicated their sentiments on an issue. Some of these sentiments might have had an impact upon the Guild's activities. For example, in the 1960 issue of the *Sundowner*, the editorial expressed what might be the main concern of the coming decade, "that of racial discrimination, with particular reference to the colour problem".[25] The editorial might not have been written by a student, but it was a portent of a period that would soon catalyse the student body. Though publications varied in what they chose to highlight, there was another observable trend: some students were conscious of the socio-politics and socio-economics of the period, reflected in articles concerning politics, economy and society. This was especially prominent in the years after 1968.

Humour and satire were one way opinions on an issue were expressed. The *Magnet* published a great deal of this kind of material. In a 1967 issue, "Con-Vice Chancellor" wrote the following:

> It is with some alarm that the author noticed the increased use that students seem to be making of the library this academic year. Perhaps this is due to the misinformation of some of our freshmen and freshettes. For their sake I issue this stern warning. Work of an academic nature must be, as far as possible, from the minds of those trying to get their degrees. It is intellectually degrading, and may threaten the tenets upon which the well-being of the student body rests. The lime is the institutionalised and well-accepted method of reaching true intellectual stature, and as academic work tends to cut drastically into liming time, every effort must be made to discourage it.[26]

In the same article:

> Two proposals were made on campus this week which deserve mention. The first concerns the national flag of Trinidad. It was proposed that its bright colours and nationalistic undertones might render it subversive. It was suggested that a photograph of Dr Williams be shown instead. The second proposal concerns Jamaica's national anthem. Owing to the singular contribution that rudie-culture and rock-steady have made to Jamaican advancement, it was suggested that the national anthem be played as a rock steady. It has been claimed by proponents of this side that the only all-pervasive entity around which to build a national culture is rock-steady. Moreover, they claim that a national anthem with a martial beat is neo-colonialist decadence, and more important, it is Un-West Indian.[27]

Noticeable were the underlying political undertones of the second quotation, which contrasts with the first. In another issue, there appeared the following letter to the editor:

> Dear Sir:
>
> I would like to protest most vigorously the non-celebration of Halloween this year in Trinidad. I warn you that such breeches [sic] of etiquette will not be countenanced by those forces for whom I write. It is an insult to every self-respecting ghost, and will hardly seem to even the most moderate spirit (if you will pardon the pun), worthy of those whom used to be. One day was all we asked. Just one little tiny evening. We slave the whole year round, and most of that on night shift, for you humans; and what do we get? We get ignored.[28]

In one of its December issues:

> We have lived too long under the tyranny of imperialistic symbols. It is time we overthrow all of the vestiges of our past degeneration and move forward into a new utopia replete with negritude and exultation of all that is West Indian. Let us batter at the bastions, one by one, until like the house built on sand, the old ways crumble into [the] forgotten, and are no more.
>
> At this time of the year, there is a particular need for us, revolutionaries. Do you realise that in a couple of weeks we will be welcoming into our homes, the very apotheosis of neo-colonialism. Who do I refer to? None other than that demonly dupe of the great powers: Santa Claus.[29]

The above articles were indicative of some students' approach to trivial matters and those of great importance. It was light-hearted but there were signs that students were aware of critical issues and expressed their feelings through humour. Perhaps there was a limit to what students felt they knew and could share on the more critical concerns, and satire, humour and poetry were some of the familiar means of remaining within accepted boundaries. Nonetheless, there were articles which gave an explicit opinion on critical concerns. Some of these were written by lecturers or academics and published for the students' benefit. Of particular interest is how some of those evolving sentiments on political and economic issues found a ready audience after 1968.

Guild's Contribution to Student Life on Campus

The start of the academic year was a period of activity for the Guild and presented the opportunity for students to familiarize themselves with their new surroundings. For the start of each year, the *Fresher's Guide* (in later years, *Freshman's Guide*) was produced by the Guild to introduce students to campus life. Becoming a member of the student body was not simply a matter of beginning classes. All new students were referred to as "grubs", and the annual "grub week" (orientation week) was a prominent feature. The list of activities for the grub week in 1967 was as follows:

> Monday – Presidential address
> Rum punch party
> Tuesday – Grub fashion parade and elimination for freshette queen contest
> Wednesday – Soul Grub Fete – Bert Bailey and the Jets
> Thursday – Freshmen's concert
> Friday – Freshman's Ball – Group solo and Dixieland steel band with crowning of the freshette queen.
> Saturday – Afternoon of sports
> Sunday – Steel band concerts

The annual carnival festivities and Christmas parties were also of some importance.

Aside from social events, the Guild sought to improve facilities for the students. In an October 1967 issue of the *Magnet*, Guild president Wilfred Phillips put forward a list of issues that the Guild council was hoping to address in the academic year. One issue was that the bar and cafeteria located at the Guild Hall were losing money; therefore, their operations were transferred to Angostura, with all profits going to the Guild.[30] Other issues included the provision of student loans, the proper care and use of the Guild's property, the appointment of a sports director, concern about the prices of books at the bookstore, availability of books, and the relationship between the bookshop proprietor and students. There was also the issue of reviving non-functioning clubs and societies. Often the issue was raised in a letter, journal or flyer, but the effort eventually subsided. If there were developments, the Guild's role in these was not clear from the documents. Be that as it may, the awareness and the effort made to create that awareness were part of the Guild's contribution towards improving students' lives.

Conclusion

The years 1962 to 1968 were defined by both evolving circumstances and entrenched continuity at the university. The Guild was able to deal with the challenges presented to it in this period and the relationship between students and the university's administration was harmonious. But conditions never remain constant, and the changes that were to come would test both the Guild and the university.

Chapter 2

Two Steps from the Maelstrom, 1968–1973

In March 1968, a new executive came to power. Suspicion immediately marred the installation of the new Guild council with regards to its election. The March 1968 issue of the *Magnet* remarked:

> Just in case there are a few people on Campus who are not aware of it, this editorial will begin by informing them that a new Guild Council was elected. Posters pasted up around the campus indicate that there are a few individuals who are at least a little disturbed by the nature of the "elections", and it is to them that this editorial is directed.
>
> Time and time again, almost ad nauseam, these editorials in the *Magnet* have stressed the gradual erosion of the democratic practices and institutions on campus. This week this campus ceased, I hope, temporarily to be a democracy. A number of individuals, in effect, appointed themselves to the Guild Council, and, with virtually no necessity to justify their claims to office, have become the student government. They may well prove a good Guild Council, and it may be that their term in office will, as they claim, mark a turning-point in Guild affairs; this will be decided by the future; but this does not alter the fact that out of a student body of over a thousand there was no effort to form an opposition.[1]

Some students involved in the politics of the Guild were concerned with this turn of events and questioned the integrity of constitutional mechanisms for elections and the effectiveness of the student body in scrutinizing representatives in the student union. Efforts at postponing the Guild elections for two weeks from its due date were unsuccessful, leading to a further cry of unfairness. While there were legitimate questions, the new council was installed with all the requisite procedures having been followed.

This council represented a turning point in the Guild's agenda of activities. The new president, Geddes Granger, was highly motivated and very determined with regard to the direction he foresaw for both Guild and university. In the heady days of the late 1960s, he symbolized a new force at the university where students were finding avenues for more forceful expression. Through print publications, meetings and demonstrations, visible action became a negotiating tool. This style of activism was not isolated, reflecting as it did the radical activity of the nation and the wider hemisphere, so that the Guild's messages were buttressed by experiences external to the university.

Contextually, by the late 1960s, the student body had grown numerically and demographically. Students of the late 1960s and early 1970s were more youthful and impatient than their predecessors of the early 1960s. The radical turn in this period was expressed in several ways, alongside the philosophy that deep concerns must be confronted. Socio-economic class and ethnic identity became significant issues in their lives. These issues were most poignantly felt by non-white students graduating from the university who perceived that opportunities within social and economic institutions were denied to them because of race or skin colour. The leftist explanation for the socio-economic relationship of those having wealth to those who struggled to make ends meet resonated with students. It was easy for students to digest messages by popular radical thinkers and activists inside and outside of UWI, such as Walter Rodney, Lloyd Best, C.L.R. James and James Millette. Nothing was lost in translation when an argument was put forward that multinational corporations owning large numbers of commercial and industrial firms in Trinidad and Tobago were directly related to the underdevelopment of the nation. Foreign ownership of local resources hamstrung the struggle to attain independence and self-rule, an argument which some students believed adequately explained the economic realities.

They were certainly exposed to this type of understanding of the regional and national socio-economic conditions. The Guild council, at least, was a leading champion of radical ideas and supporter of radical personalities beginning with the 1968–69 Guild council. The connection the Guild shared with such ideas was especially evident in some of the events that occurred in 1968, one of which involved an alumnus of UWI. The popular Guyanese lecturer at Mona, Walter Rodney, who graduated from UWI in 1963, used an analysis of class and race to highlight the injustices within English-speaking Caribbean society. In 1968, he was to return to Jamaica after attending the Montreal Conference of Black Writers in October of that year. However, the Jamaican government viewed him as a "grave security risk" and barred his re-entry to the country.[2] Students at the Mona campus immediately responded and protested the decision by the Jamaican government. Soon after, there were reactions by the Guild of Students at the Cave Hill and St Augustine campuses to the barring of Rodney.

Whereas the problem of earlier years was low student participation, this period was marked by heightened student radicalism and awareness, at least in the way envisioned by activists. But it must also be understood that this movement was not of the entire student body, which serves as an important point of context. Radicalism was confined to a few and, indeed, there were students who opposed the activities of the Guild council before and after the Rodney incident. Nevertheless, the unfolding drama of the radicals speaks to a dimension of the student body eager for change.

This had an impact upon the Guild council's activities and the role it played in the life of students as well as the university. The student versus administration conflict, for example, represented the powerless versus the powerful, a binary which submissions to the Guild publications were eager to point out. Dialectics was the popular underlying explanation used by student radicals to articulate the way society, economics, politics and the university operated. As a consequence, the adoption of radical resolutions by the Guild was done to alert those in authority of the strength of the student body.

Geddes Granger (Makandal Daaga)

Perhaps no individual so fittingly symbolized this era of change that was to come to the Guild and the university as a whole than did the president for the academic year 1968–69, Geddes Granger. He grew up in one of Trinidad and Tobago's depressed areas, Laventille. Roy Mitchell describes the familial background of Granger as "materially poor but spiritually rich".[3] It was a humble upbringing for Granger, whose hard-working mother did everything she could to support her children, even the "adopted" ones.⁴ Granger's background did not stymie his drive for educational achievement. He was a scholarship winner, which allowed him to attend one of the more prestigious schools in the country, St Mary's College. Upon graduating, Granger went on to work for the Ministry of Works and later on the Ministry of Finance, Planning and Development.

Following independence in 1962, Granger found many outlets for his social activism. This involvement hinged on his worldviews, one of which was the promotion of a strong, locally generated cultural presence through the arts. He also espoused the need to change the socio-economic relationships of nation, in which the colonial legacies of race, class and colour still lingered. In 1962, Granger formed a movement called Pegasus, inspired by the winged horse in Greek mythology. Mitchell describes Pegasus as "an inspiration, a movement, a spirit from which great things would have been expected for Trinidad and Tobago".⁵

Upon its establishment, the Pegasus focused on artists, attempting to blend the nation's diverse cultural and artistic forms into a cohesive interrelationship. It was believed that through art, an independent nation would achieve its goals and dreams. To this end, local artists were recruited to stage cultural events. But staging cultural events was one thing, and Granger felt that recognition had to take on more tangible and prestigious forms. He devised a national awards committee to honour the nation's outstanding artists, such as Vidia Naipaul, Beryl McBurnie, Carlisle Chang and C.L.R. James. Reflecting on his efforts, Granger noted, "I felt that Independence must mean something more to the people than the ceremony at Queen's Park Savannah. The people were not involved enough, so that some way had to be found to give our people pride and a sense of history. So we came up with the idea of not only honouring our artistes, but also our national heroes."⁶

University

When Granger entered UWI, he was older than the average student and had a long résumé of social activism behind him. In 1966, he was the Faculty of Arts and Science representative on the Guild council, which made him a prominent figure on the St Augustine campus. Mitchell noted, "Geddes was now pitched into a situation where he was serving two masters, Pegasus, his brainchild and the Guild of Undergraduates of UWI his adopted child."7 In March 1968, he became president of the Guild. Aiyegoro Ome stated that upon Granger's appointment, a redefinition of the role of the university and the student on campus was explored. In the 1968 issue of the *Pelican*, five points spelled out what the university's role should be:

1. To train its students in the various spheres of knowledge relevant to the particular society.
2. To develop among its students the spirit of critical knowledge and objective approach in pursuit of knowledge.
3. To extend the frontiers of knowledge and human experience.
4. To be the conscience of the society in which it exists.
5. To be the herald of progress and meaningful change.8

These were lofty goals, given the frequent complaints of student apathy in earlier years. But the turn towards student radicalism represented a changed dynamic among a section of the student body.

Granger's year as president was filled with incident. At every opportunity, he challenged the university establishment on issues he felt were crucial to students' interests. National and international circumstances created new opportunities for him to galvanize opinion. His goal was to have relevant social issues at the forefront of the university's agenda. Some of his requests were simple, such as turning the Guild Hall into a cultural centre. In a letter responding to Granger's proposal, pro vice chancellor and principal Dudley Huggins wrote, "At the meeting of staff and students yesterday, you raised the question of converting the existing guild hall into a cultural centre. The idea seems to me a good one but we need to counsel together about what we have in mind and how to bring about something which is of optimum service to the community and particularly the university community."9 Other decisions were more complicated and forceful, such as the storming by Granger and Guild council members of the principal's office, demanding better accommodation at the soon-to-be-completed John F. Kennedy (JFK) Complex in early October 1968.10

Much as the Guild council sought to rally students and the university to action, however, the administration did not present itself as a counterforce but instead attempted to maintain close contact with the Guild. In correspondence between Huggins and the Guild's executive, the principal expressed his concern about student affairs and his wish to have monthly meetings with the executive. The problem was perhaps that the gap between lip service and real action frustrated many; and for an eager Granger, the pace of developments was certainly slow.

Granger was joined by a cadre of young, strong-willed individuals who shared his views on the condition of the university and society. They included Dave D'Arbeau (later Khafra Kambon), David Murray (later Aiyegoro Ome), Augustus Ramrekersingh (Guild secretary) and Syl Lowhar (EAC chairman). Tutored by university and social intellectuals on the ideas of race and class relationships as important forces in Caribbean society, they were also led to adopt radical approaches to alter the historical conditions that entrenched these relationships. Murray, for example, wrote in the *Vanguard* of March 1970 that "while thousands of people joined the historic March to Caroni it was apparent that there is still considerable ignorance of the lives of the African who came here as a slave and that the East Indian brother joined the society as an indentured servant . . . Fewer still are aware of the serious implications of colonial disunity of we Black people."[11]

Syl Lowhar, reflecting on the Black Power movement, poetically describes the context and reveals his sentiment at the time: "I remember as a child seeing blacks driven from pews to make way for those who could afford to pay – they had to pay to worship. They have faced discrimination in the Courts of Justice. The moment a black man walks into a court, he is divested of his respectability and his manhood, his name is shouted as though he is a common dog."[12] Granger's consciousness of the radical events of Afro-Trinidadian history was also reflected in the renaming of Guild Hall as Daaga Hall, after the African leader of the 1837 mutiny at St Joseph. Granger would later adopt the name Daaga as his surname.

October 1968 stands out as the preeminent month in Granger's tenure. The Walter Rodney incident drew considerable attention to Granger's actions and placed the Guild and the campus at the forefront of national consciousness. Like their counterparts at Mona and Cave Hill, the St Augustine Guild organized its own demonstration in a show of mutual support by marching to Port of Spain. Petitions were presented to the Jamaican high commission and to Trinidad and Tobago's prime minister, Eric Williams. This show of force was greeted warmly by intellectuals and students within the university, as well as by the media.

Buttressed by this new-found popularity, the Guild was once again in the limelight a few months later in February 1969, this time regarding the detention of Caribbean students at the Sir George Williams University in Canada in August 1968. The governor general of Canada, Roland Michener, on an official visit to the St Augustine campus, was greeted by a group of 150 students holding placards protesting the injustice faced by the Caribbean students at the Sir George Williams University. He and his entourage, which included Eric Williams, were prevented from entering the campus. This protest, however, was not viewed favourably and did not gain widespread support, unlike the earlier demonstration that erupted in support of Walter Rodney. There was a level of national embarrassment as both the media and politicians felt that the Guild and the students had gone too far in blocking the governor general's entry.

Granger was an exception to the rule at UWI, given his socio-economic background, social activism and compelling persona. Opinions about him are wide-ranging, portraying him as either hero or villain. But Granger embodies the paradox in history of being both a hero and an anti-hero, a pioneering as well as a maligned figure. Two intriguing editorial excerpts in the *Canadian* highlight this paradox. In March 1969, the editorial commented that

> Geddes Granger on his way down has been clutching at straws, he has as usual been clouding issues in his loquacious ramblings, on, and more often than not off the topic being discussed. It is quite an experience to hear Geddes' discourse, quite an exercise in how well we can cover up an issue by bringing others less significant; or by distorting the original one so much that we doubt its former significance. And quite in context, and we may add quite in character, this is what Geddes has done.[13]

A year later, another *Canadian* editorial remarked that

> within the last fourteen months the University of the West Indies has undergone a considerable transformation. We witnessed the meteoric rise of [the] Geddes Granger faction to unprecedented power and publicity – prodded by the Rodney and Michener affairs – and then the gradual withering away of Geddes Granger from the campus political arena, though his intermittent visits at times of crisis leaves me to wonder as to his next move.
>
> Undoubtedly Geddes Granger et al. have done a lot of good for the student body by demanding the respect and grudging cooperation of the administration. However, in achieving their objectives they have presented the university in a very unfavourable

light to the public and have thrived on cheap sensationalism propagated by frothy journalism. This disintegration of the Geddes Granger guild council left some of us with a taste of happiness and relief – others with a taste of remorse and futility. However, it certainly paved the way for a bright future, which unfortunately has been fraught with irrational, emotional, and disgusting incidents.[14]

The 1970 editorial succinctly captured Granger's tenure, understanding that he shaped the direction of the student body for another generation while at the same time exciting the vitriol of many as a result of being at the forefront.

In March 1969, Granger vacated office and his successor, Jamaican student Carl Blackwood, presided over a small but highly politicized group of students connecting with radical forces outside the university. Blackwood engineered a style of activism of his own that took the Guild to the streets. February 1970 stands as the pivotal moment in national and Guild history, as the Black Power movement connected with the consciousness of the students and the nation. The march to Port of Spain and the march to Caroni became symbolic acts showing how far radicalism had come.

Deepening the Social Context

While Granger represented a turn to social radicalism, it is important to appreciate the hemispheric and regional convulsions which gave added dimension to the activities of Granger and those around him. Bridget Brereton notes, "the region was not immune from world-wide trends towards student politicisation and militancy so salient in the 1960s, and the civil rights struggles in the USA had also been very influential, as well as the Cuban Revolution and related events in Latin America".[15]

In 1968, the Civil Rights movement in the United Sates gained momentum following the assassinations of Martin Luther King Jr and Malcolm X, as African Americans empowered through civil pressure forced changes. Trinidad-born Stokely Carmichael made his presence felt in the United States with his radical activity, and his use of the phrase Black Power accelerated the term's use. Simultaneously, tertiary-level student movements in the United States brought pressure on political forces in the United States on such issues as the Vietnam War, women's rights and youth subculture.

African American and African Caribbean identity experienced a sense of growth and change as the intellectual culture of black identity took shape. The Congress of Black Writers in Montreal, Canada, in 1968 was a seminal gathering of intellectuals, with many key personalities from the Caribbean and North America exploring the issues of pan-Africanism and black identity which testified to the strength of the movement. Attending this conference were leading intellectuals such as Carmichael, James Forman, Harry Edwards, C.L.R. James, Richard B. Moore, Walter Rodney and Robert Hill.

The search for black identity was pursued in the midst of the ideologically polarized world brought on by Cold War politics and the struggle of colonial and post-colonial states against their imperial masters. These anti-colonial struggles, symbolized through revolutionary activities in Latin America, Africa, the Middle East and the Far East, represented the intensifying battle for underdeveloped societies. The view that political and territorial decolonization did not destroy the legacies of economic, social, cultural and psychological colonialism created vigilant anti-colonialist movements wary of metropolitan multinational corporations and foreign experts spouting formulas for economic development.

Closer to home, there was a small movement of youth activism led by Michael Als, in Trinidad and Tobago, who spoke on the politics and social issues of young people. There were also small groups subscribing to teacher power, women power and even Christian power. The nation was certainly full of groups wanting empowerment.

The Sir George Williams University incident was also crucial. Caribbean students attending that university complained of the unfair treatment they received, especially the grading of a particular lecturer. The complaints were ignored and the students conducted a sit-in protest at the computer laboratory of the university to highlight their concerns. It led to a confrontation between the Caribbean students and authorities with items in the laboratory being destroyed by fire as a result. The students were arrested and put on trial. Since the Caribbean students were non-white, it was viewed as an example of the era's ongoing concerns about racism.

The UWI was not immune to this activity. The ideologies and messages being transmitted were shared concerns of the societies of the Caribbean and would also have shaped the thinking of the students at all three campuses. It is against this backdrop that the Black Power movement of 1970 became a culminating event of the era.

The Maelstrom

The activities of the year 1970 were visible by-products of the stronger student consciousness that was encouraged by leading radical intellectuals. In the late 1960s, the university was one of the major centres where radicalism found ready acceptance, based as it was on ideas of racial and ancestral identity, socio-economic justice, and political transformation. Following the ascension of Granger, this radicalism took the shape of publications, demonstrations, meetings and idealistic agendas of changing society.

In the 1969 issue of the *Vanguard*, Dave D'Arbeau wrote on the issue of Rodney's travel prohibition and the problems with lecturing appointments at the university:

> The university, if it is to justify its existence in this society, cannot continue to be the monastic, detached training camp for teachers and civil servants which it has been in the past for quite understandable reasons. The actions of the regional governments are unfortunately reinforcing the tendency for detached, mainly irrelevant academic pursuits in the University. The lecturers who find themselves in difficulty are generally young West Indians with creative minds whose major crime is relevance to the society. The policy-making Committee of the University Council is dominated not only by politicians, but by political interests. Council has become therefore just another expression of all the pettiness and insularity which plague Caribbean politics.[16]

The article went on: "Rodney and [Clive Y.] Thomas are lost to UWI temporarily at least; Rodney like thousands of others in that anonymous crowd called the 'Brain Drain' is lost to the region. But the lessons they have taught us are indelible. We may well feel hopeless in the situation. We may recognize that ultimately the survival of the university will depend on our ability to effect revolutionary change in the society."[17] However, it is important to emphasize the extent of this student radicalism. It was limited and the apathy of previous years remained ever present. But it was unlikely that any student would have been unaware of the issues being discussed. Kambon, for example, claims that 75 to 90 per cent of the student body participated in the Rodney demonstration in Port of Spain on 17 October 1968.[18] This figure seems highly unlikely given the already frequent complaints of student apathy.

Be that as it may, the events of February and March 1970 were a turning point. On 26 February 1970, the Guild joined with the recently founded

National Joint Action Committee, led by Geddes Granger and a few other radical elements, in a protest demonstration against the trial of the Caribbean students in Canada. They marched to the Canadian high commission, the Roman Catholic cathedral, and the Royal Bank of Canada. While many understood the plight of youth, with even A.N.R. Robinson welcoming the "new mood" among youth,[19] acceptance of such demonstrations was inevitably sapped when newspapers reported on the actions of the protestors at the cathedral. Some of the cathedral's effigies were "desecrated" when black cloths were used to cover their faces and their arms were used to hang signs. An *Express* editorial remarked, "The time has come when they must pause and ask themselves whether they are making enough of a distinction between the importance of demonstrating for a cause which is a dignified act and the overspill into exhibitionism into which they so easily get carried away."[20]

Analytically, the movement was seen as lacking purpose, as an editorial in the *Guardian* observed: "In expressing their dissatisfaction, the dissenters have so far not been able to articulate quite properly the precise causes of their discontent, have hurled justifiable and unjustifiable accusations all around and have exposed a very explosive situation which can do irreparable harm to the black power advocates, to the country, and to the cause itself."[21] Five were held in custody following the demonstration: Russell Andalcio, Blackwood (president of the Guild), D'Arbeau, Granger and Winston Smart; all were subsequently released after being granted bail. The Guild had its own response to the actions the police took against the protestors, as reported by the *Express*:

> It seems as though those who were calling for justice for their fellow nationals in Canada were treated as if the offences which they allegedly committed were more serious than those of their compatriots in Canada, and this by a supposedly black government.
>
> We refer to the harsh treatment handed down by the police and the brutal manner in which the arrests were made.
>
> ... the march showed the intensity of feeling on the part of the nation's young people against racism and foreign exploitation.[22]

Early March saw a wave of protest outside of the university, which lent credibility to the demonstrations. But most important was the indication that Trinidad and Tobago's society was reeling from the effects of difficult socio-economic relationships.

After these months of frenetic activity (February–April 1970), demonstrations waned, but the movement left a lasting legacy. Granger had changed the image of the Guild president as well as of what the Guild council could do. His immediate successors attempted to capture the spirit and energy that he brought to his role, with some adopting his radical rhetoric. The era piqued the consciousness of students, making them aware of social, cultural and economic issues. Awareness of the issues evoked confrontational responses, but, later on, other avenues for expression as well as changing economic circumstances allowed more constructive responses to emerge. This was seen in the growth of student groups or societies exploring ethnic, racial or ancestral identities using intellectual and historical perspectives. Finally, the university's establishment also changed, no longer having the conventions of the pre-1968 period. The message of left-leaning ideology began to seep in, changing the university's place in the wider society.

Radicalized Publications

Reflecting the shift towards radicalization were the types of articles that appeared in the Guild's publications as well as in those of other student groups circulated on campus. Broadly, articles that were anti-establishment appeared in almost every issue, other articles explored the role of the student, while others reflected on radicalism or new ideologies.

One of the more consistent campus publications that adopted the radical style was the journal *Embryo*, which was launched in 1967 and produced by the publications committee of the Guild. For example, an article titled "Wanted: A Revolution" stated, "Life is revolution. Visible progress rises from the translation of creative thought into some meaningful form whereby it could be understood. A revolution cannot be transplanted. It may be encouraged by a few, but it happens to the many. Rebels are either buried in Bolivian anonymity, muzzled by Soviet or harassed in Red-Guard Cultural Revolution."[23] Another article read, "What then of students? The fact is that the future of UWI rests squarely on our shoulders. For with the Govts [*sic*] of the region pressurizing an impotent administration; and with Administration in turn dictating to staff, the only area of resistance lies with the student body. Generally speaking our response has not been good enough."[24]

The journal also carried the introduction by Adolfo Gilly, an Argentinian intellectual, to Frantz Fanon's *Dying Colonialism*. This is poignant because of its reference to revolution, as follows: "Revolution is mankind's way of life today. This is the age of revolution; the age of indifference is gone forever . . . Humanity has erupted violently, tumultuously into the stage of history, taking its own destiny in its hands. Capitalism is under siege, surrounded by a global tidal wave of revolution."[25] But radicalism was one part of this changing consciousness, socio-cultural awareness was another. *Embryo* became a forum for socio-cultural concerns, including concerns of the Hindu-Indian community on campus. On 4 December 1970, Surujrattan Rambachan, a former president of the UWI student group the Society for the Propagation of Indian Culture (SPIC), responded to an article written by Maurice Gonzalves that appeared in the *Guardian* a few days earlier that pushed forward the idea that Indians were "separatists". Rambachan delivered a scathing reply:

> But I issue a warning to Mr. Gonzalves and to all those other folk who delight in criticising us. We as Hindus and Indians, more so have had it! We shall no longer tolerate your denigration, scorn and contempt of our culture and religious tenets. We shall no longer be "token" elements (like the Woodstock committee on Campus will tell you). We want equality, justice and impartiality in treatment, in facilities. Recognise our existence, recognise our presence, recognise our needs for if you don't we are going to seek it out – at all costs.[26]

While Rambachan's article sounded a hostile note, others used the medium to express constructive or conscious views on the Indian community such as J.C. Jha, Brinsley Samaroo, Winston Krishna Gannessingh and Kenneth Parmasad. Parmasad responded to a letter by Yusuf Omatunde, saying, "Our inmost creed should be to find the one humanity in the many. Our salvation lies in the unity not in the uniformity of our diverse peoples. We must not admit differences to be conflict, nor must we espy an enemy in every stranger. We must try to find a place for all in a vast social field."[27] Indian cultural consciousness was just one aspect of socio-cultural awareness as champions of Africans, Chinese, Christians, Muslims, Hindus and women wrote to the journal.

The *Magnet*, the *Canadian* and *Insight* were other publications of a fairly radical nature. In the wake of the Rodney affair, the *Magnet* of November 1968 published an article on student power:

"Student power" is a phrase that conjures up pictures of militant, bearded young would-be intellectuals brandishing placards and taking part in sometimes violent demonstrations.

But in Nova Scotia, the idea of student power is being calmly pursued by both students and administration in many of the province's colleges.

The presidents of Dalhousie, Acadia, King's, St Francis Xavier and St Mary's universities in Nova Scotia have agreed that students should have a voice in matters concerning them.[28]

In the *Insight* of 1974, Bill Riviere, a former lecturer in the Department of History at UWI, who was one of two St Augustine lecturers detained in 1970 and subsequently deported to his home country of Dominica, wrote as follows:

> Comrade brothers and sisters at St Augustine, the University of the West Indies has a vital role to play in this catalysis of the struggle for revolutionary change that has been in progress for some time in the Caribbean . . . but far less certain is the methodology on the basis of which a mind severely exhausted by the hopes and despairs, consistencies and contradictions of October to now can, within the period of time between today and your *Embryo*'s going to press, deal competently with an analysis of that role.[29]

In an article in the *Canadian*, the author spoke about the Black Power movement, clearly defining its purpose, and went on to state that "we need a changed social order, we need a new economic system. Let us therefore, all of us who claim to be radicals and revolutionaries, get down to the task of drafting that new system. The blueprints must be discussed by the society. Some of the ground work must be done, there is very much more to be done."[30] One prescription to the difficult socio-economic conditions was to overhaul the social, economic and political system as recommended by a writer in the *Arts Annual*:

> What we need is a Radical Social, Economic and Political change. It is evident that there has been a profound psychological awakening. This is good. We need a change of Government and a change of system. If we only change the Government and not the system we will be merely effecting a palace Revolution, synonymous with our Latin American neighbours.
>
> Therefore, "What is to be done?" Unless the present trend is reversed or halted the system will generate further discontent and more violent upheavals. This would

either lead to repressive regimes, still trying to work on anachronistic models, or to a blossoming of one party states. Moreover the present parliamentary system must be substantially modified to suit local needs.[31]

Publications therefore shifted in what they presented to students and what they felt students were most inclined to read. While many were short-lived, publications did produce an impact, though much more gradual than revolutionary.

Radical students therefore used a double-pronged approach to try to stimulate action – protest and publications. The goal of publications was to create an environment of awareness so that action would be forthcoming. It is also important to recognize another important nuance. Students within the university felt powerless against larger establishment forces, and confrontation was the tool used by many powerless groups to highlight a cause or to seek resolution on a particular issue. The result was that publications in which students vented their feelings abounded. Students and student groups may not have shared the same ideology or philosophy, but they often shared the same style of action. It created a dynamic and highly charged environment, which found radical students within the Guild council in the enviable position of championing various issues.

Constitutional Transformation in an Era of Radicalism

The speedy pace of developments on the ground did not allow room for constitutional concerns. Granger's main focus while in office was social activism rather than constitutional matters. It was in 1971, under the presidency of Sheridan Gregoire, that constitutional reform was once again brought to the table. A number of proposals were forwarded to the secretary of UWI St Augustine, Hugh Gibson, on 23 October 1971. Four main areas were explored: clearly defining the relationship between the Guild and clubs and societies; nomination of chairpersons to committees of the Guild; the insertion of the power of recall at all levels of the Guild; and increasing student participation in the Guild through constitutional reform.

In addition to this, a proposed restructuring of the Guild, the Guild committees, clubs and societies was considered. An organizational chart was submitted with proposals which called for three levels: the lower level comprising the clubs and societies, sports and games organizations, a faculty council where representatives of each faculty were elected, representatives of the halls of residence and EAC representatives; above this, a second level narrowing further the representation from the level below; and at the top level, the students' council with elected and nominated posts, including key positions such as treasurer, secretary, chairman and permanent secretary. There was a right of recall for all positions. A note to these proposals suggested a two-week election period when each level of the Guild would be voted in.[32]

It was a confusing and contradictory proposal which was not well thought out. The need for it was answered within the proposal itself in a section titled "Why a New Structure":

> Well, what's wrong with the old, still existing one?
> You will need to know first of all what the old structure is.
> Most students have probably only a vague notion of how the Guild of which they are members operates.
> While there is on this campus a department of political science which is constantly studying the constitutions by which countries are governed, how many students have read, or know anything at all about the constitution under which their affairs are conducted.
> This perhaps is the first, most obvious, indication that the present constitution – and the manner in which student affairs are conducted are in need of reappraisal.
> People don't know what's going on. They don't even know if anything is going on. Why? Because it seems the present system permits people to feel they are not a part of it.[33]

Upon receiving the proposal, Gibson requested that specific areas of the constitution be addressed and that it go to the Campus Academic Board, instead of to the senate, which had never approved a Guild constitution, in a meeting scheduled for 25 November 1971.[34] The proposal seen by the academic board had the modifications recommended by Gibson. The specific areas of change were outlined:

> SPECIFIC AREAS OF CHANGE IN THE CONSTITUTION BEFORE:
> President, Vice President, Secretary, Treasurer, Guild Hall Secretary, Guild Hall Treasurer, Games Committee Chairman, Inter-Clubs Committee Chairman and External Affairs Chairman were all elected by the general student body.
> NOW: President, Secretary and Treasurer only will be elected by the general student body.

> The Games Committee chairman will be elected by the Games Committee.
> The ICC Chairman will be elected by the ICC. The EAC Chairman will be elected by the EAC.
> The Chairman and Treasurer of the Student Union will be appointed by the Student Council.
> There shall be no election for Vice President, but the Secretary shall automatically be the First Vice President, and the Treasurer, the second Vice President.
> The Secretary of the Student Union shall be appointed by the Union Committee (formerly known as the Guild Hall Committee).
> BEFORE: The Guild Year was from 1st March to 28/29 February.
> NOW: The Guild Year is from 1st December to 30th November.
> NOW: The Guild Councillors are subject to recall by the group which elected them, e.g. the Games Committee Chairman, by the Games Committee.

The interesting part of the proposal was the power of recall, which was felt to be crucial for dealing with ineffective and inefficient Guild councillors, the presence of whom was becoming a problem as councillors were being elected to positions but not fulfilling their roles and responsibilities. During the 1970s, by-elections occurred often in the Guild, with four presidents being changed via by-elections during that decade. While the record is not clear as to the reasons, these proposals were not followed through, for by 1977, Gibson, writing to Professor A.R. Carnegie at Cave Hill, Barbados, stated that the Guild was still operating under the 1965 draft proposal constitution.[35]

Other Concerns of the Guild

While the Guild was engaged in radical activity, it also had other concerns. During this period, Guild's focus was divided between addressing the concerns of the student body and connecting with society in a meaningful way. Mention has been made of Granger's effort to create these types of connections. Both socio-cultural activism and conventional student activities were prominent features. The latter included sporting, cultural and academic activities. For example, the Inter-Campus Committee (ICC) occasionally held debates as part of ICC week, a UWI-wide event. A St Augustine contingent was usually present at this event.

In July 1968, the Guild hosted the Yale University choir at St Mary's College, Port of Spain, which was a collaborative initiative. In August 1968, an informal meeting of the Guild with Pro Vice Chancellor Huggins raised the issue of encouraging greater appreciation by students of sporting and other extra-curricular activities. In April 1970, the pro vice chancellor was invited by the Guild to a variety arts concert at the JFK lecture theatre which was held in aid of a trip by a few students to the Cave Hill campus to attend an artistic event. Later that year, efforts were made to reach out to communities. An example of one of these initiatives was an invitation by the EAC to residents of Erin, a small village in the south of Trinidad, to visit the campus for a day and use the facilities. Student clubs and societies made greater efforts to seek sponsorship from the Guild for their events and activities such as debates, Christmas choir visits to underprivileged children's homes, and sporting activities. Finally, in August 1973, the steelpan group Birdsong was established after months of effort.

While these efforts were small in scale compared to some others, they represented the diverse agenda of the Guild council and may have allowed students less inclined to radicalism the opportunity to participate in volunteer activity. Diversity had always been part of the campus committee; however, consistent participation was not. Therefore, single events such as these during the height of radicalism indicate that the student body was not monolithic and there was a varied dimension.

Conclusion

The period from 1968 to 1973 marks a transition point at which the Guild of Students became more meaningful and relevant. It was less of a closed nexus representing student interests and had begun to take on an outreach role within the university and the wider society. This marked one era of the Guild which led to the opening up of a new age in the Guild's short history.

Chapter 3

Redirecting Radical Consciousness, 1973–1980

The Black Power movement transformed the national landscape while the UWI underwent its fair share of transformation. The Guild of Students adopted a different ethos after the early 1970s, becoming more confrontational in its communications with establishment forces, while being more critical and suspicious in its outlook on socio-economic issues. As well, the ideals and causes the Guild chose to represent had also changed. By the mid-1970s, student radicals were less visible on the streets (or in this case, on campus), turning instead to print media. Those who had not done so before were now using publications to express ideologies and opinions or to vent frustration over a specific concern.

Context

Students entering UWI were ambitious, based on the reasonable expectation that opportunities would become available after long years of study. From 1968 to 1973, awareness of social and economic issues had an impact on how students perceived these opportunities; for some, circumstances appeared bleak, but the economic environment by the mid-1970s was one of optimism. Rich in petroleum, Trinidad and Tobago became a leading industrial nation in the region, a fate that other nations did not enjoy. Political forces played a role, as the vision of Prime Minister Eric Williams enabled Trinidad and Tobago to capitalize on the emerging economic opportunities. The oil sector received a boost when world prices rose dramatically, resulting in enormous revenues from petroleum exportation from 1973 to 1981, during the first oil boom.

According to Bridget Brereton, this was a boon to the Faculty of Engineering in particular, as its interests were closely tied to that of the political administration. The expertise of engineers was directed towards the development of the national energy sector and the infrastructure, thus elevating the faculty above other faculties and departments. Overall though, the university as a whole benefited from this extra attention. The resulting economic stimulation from greater exports of petroleum and petroleum-based products and the high oil prices between 1973 and 1981 enhanced the government's ability to fund the university. This meant expansion of facilities as well as greater opportunities for students.

The impact was visible in the deradicalization of the student militancy that had marked earlier years. If one of the glaring problems confronting young people in earlier years was lack of opportunity, the new economic prosperity meant there were now opportunities for employment and financial rewards. As also observed later on, the administration of UWI was then able to tackle the perceived student detachment, leading to greater student involvement in the administrative processes.

The impact of these developments was concurrently felt by the Guild. While there remained a radical spirit, especially among those on the Guild council, which was by and large difficult to root out, the Guild as a whole was less inclined to summon the students to action. Therefore, it shifted its focus to publications and to encouraging greater student consciousness. There was greater awareness of ethnic, social and racial issues, and these years saw the rise of student groups where students of Indian, African, Islamic, Roman Catholic and Hindu backgrounds created avenues to express their ancestral and cultural heritage. One example of this can be observed in the publication *Lotus*, by SPIC. The society was established in 1969 and its goals were to disseminate information and promote Indian culture and Indian cultural activities. Notably, the mid-1970s saw the inauguration of the Conferences on East Indians in the Caribbean by academics at the St Augustine campus, held to discuss issues of diasporic and Caribbean Indians.

Students of African ancestry also developed greater appreciation of African culture and heritage. While promoting this heritage and culture was a feature of the 1960s, a new phase was entered, in which Afro-themed images were promoted for the orientation of young people. The discourse of self-appreciation had become important and was reflected in what music one listened to, how one dressed, the cultural events one attended, and how one perceived race. Through its publications, the Guild actively promoted these images and the result was a gradual transformation of students' thinking.

Therefore, the campus was less stifled by the conventions, traditions, or prejudices of the past, as evident in the disposition of Lloyd Braithwaite, principal of the St Augustine campus (1969–85), who wore casual attire and was student friendly.[1] According to Brereton, he preferred academics to administration and was especially keen on regional issues.

Student numbers were also on the rise, though less dramatically than in previous years, and the demographic shifted to a younger, more racially diverse and more energetic student body. Therefore, the range of activities for student participation was greater, to cater to diverse student tastes. Those inclined towards sports had numerous sporting activities from which to choose, while those academically or culturally oriented also had opportunities for participation. These years also saw the development of placement services for students transitioning from university to the job market, which eased the students' entry into the world of work.

Contextually, these changes emerged after a period of radicalism, and further developments were taking place in this ongoing radical spirit. A compromise was reached between the Guild of Students and the university on the type of transformation that had occurred.

Publications as a Forum of Expression

Embryo was a popular forum of expression. Though it was not stated explicitly, many of its contributors were sympathetic to issues of the working class and inclined towards socialist, anti-colonial and anti-imperialist ideology. These sympathies were reflected in the journal's choice of material for publication that was along the lines of extreme political, cultural or economic nationalism, which at times conflicted with the Guild council's viewpoints. A few telling examples are illustrative. An article titled "Unity, Imperialism, and Cricket" observed that "the university has suffered from an archaic administrative framework, within which dishonest and spineless intellectuals operate. These owe their positions and privileges, and are therefore subservient to corrupt and repressive island governments who in turn, kowtow and worship before the word issuing from Washington and London, like the true neo-colonial puppets they are."[2] In another article in support of Cuba's revolutionary struggle, one writer referred to the inspiration that the Cuban experience provided to the region:

> Cuba teaches us that our problems which were the same that they had can be solved, inspite of our being underdeveloped in spite [sic] of US aid and [the] Guantanamo base, Cuba teaches us by example that politicians can be honest, that economists and politicians can make mistakes, admit them and still remain great, that serious planning entails a total knowledge of one's economy, that the multinational corporations and those who support or collaborate with them are enemies of underdeveloped countries, that a new breed of men conscious and determined must be produced to change our societies, that tinkering with and tailoring our Caribbean economies will not solve economic problems, that unemployment can be solved, that class analysis is relevant in the Caribbean, that socialism is the only answer that will solve our problems.[3]

Finally, another article, "Elections in Perspective", on the general elections of 1976 in Trinidad and Tobago, stated that

> around elections time all the forces of the ruling classes are gathered to ensure that the "fittest" reaches the tape ahead of the field. And in this situation the press and the campaign financiers (capitalist enterprises) and of course the CIA play a significant part. Which of us will not forget the campaign in the press against Allende of Chile and the CIA and ITT instigated fascist coup on his Government?[4]

These articles were the residue of the early 1970s' radicalism. But by the late 1970s, the radical element had declined and most of the articles featured in *Embryo* were analogous to those of the pre-1968 period. Articles concerning student interests, Guild operations, human interest stories, events on the international stage or cultural developments began to be published. Overall, as well, the publication was reduced, with fewer pages and issues being produced each year. Volume 3, which ran from 5 October 1970 to 29 April 1971, had nineteen issues, with each edition running to a dozen pages or more. Volume 14, however, had eight issues, from October 1981 to May 1982, with some having fewer than five pages. This was indicative of the changing consciousness of students as well as the points of focus for incoming Guild councils.

While *Embryo* served as one popular forum, there were other outlets where students expressed a point of view. Students for Change was a group that produced a radical publication in the vein of anti-imperialism, cultural nationalism and working-class sympathies. Some articles centred on radical approaches to resolving socio-economic dilemmas. In looking at the influence of American music on Trinbago's youth, an editorial recommended that "youths and students of Trinbago, these songs, the products of the 'funk factories' do not belong to us. This music is part of the culture of the imperialists and their comprador lackeys. The content of the music is the content of all imperialistic culture-individualism, selfishness, and greed. Such values are not the values of the oppressed people of the world."[5] Another declared:

> We, in Trinidad and Tobago, live in a neo-colonial, capitalist state, dominated on the economic front by US imperialist investment and politically controlled by their comprador descendants of the house-slaves, the chosen few of the "Massah." The politico-economic control of the new imperialist rulers of Trinbago extends to the sphere of education. Here, from Standard I, through the GCE distortion of History, to the final sophistication of UWI, the imperialist machine prepares us as graduates "certified" to be defenders of imperialist interest, as apologists for neo-colonialism.[6]

In October 1976, the group put forward a manifesto, stating, "The ultimate goal of the organization is to build a strong and vibrant anti-imperialist student organization through the involvement of students in our activities."[7] Some students involved in the arts or culture also displayed ideologically radical thinking, since they perhaps felt the greatest pressure from Western cultural forms. An article in the *Voice of the Hermits*[8] suggested that the university remained colonially inclined: "The university is still a colonial institution founded by metropolitan interest and contributing very little towards the process of decolonization and the advancement of the Caribbean. This colonial educational system merely serves the purpose of perpetuating the status quo and has very little relevance to the needs of the Caribbean."[9] In *Riteflow*, a publication produced for the second Annual Festival of Arts, Craft, and Literature at the St Augustine campus, an article highlighted the neglect of kaiso music: "The influx of foreign music on our airwaves creates an almost chronic problem in the form of indoctrinating the youths towards a taste for foreign music. The Black Power Movement of the early seventies has created an awareness among our people for 'black' music and the only black music exposed to us via the mass media (radio especially) are [*sic*] soul music from America and reggae music from Jamaica."[10]

While not all students embraced radical ideology, those who did found it a means of connecting with peers. The Guild, through its publications committee, tapped into this sentiment and helped disseminate information or ideas through its journals. The result was a literary radicalism rather than physical activism; though this is not to say that activism was dead. Literary radicalism signalled a different approach to how the Guild council operated and its effect on students. It also transformed the relationship with the university's administration, as will be seen later on.

Supporting Strikes by Non-academic Staff

While active radicalism had subsided considerably, there were moments when some students embraced a call to action in support of a particular concern. In 1973, at the Mona campus in Jamaica, non-academic workers who went on strike for better wages were supported by the Guild of Students. As proponents of the reality of working class exploitation, students supported non-academic staff through protest demonstrations or voiced their concerns in publications. Similar action was seen at St Augustine, as well, when workers went on strike in 1973. The Guild of Students immediately lent its support and showed its solidarity with the workers, as shown in the following excerpt from an article published in the *Embryo*:

> I cannot but notice the plight of the non-academic worker on this campus in addition to his daily struggles against Admin. Every effort seems bent on keeping the worker from using the facilities of the University to the fullest extent. Many workers (if not all) do not use the library facilities, not even to read the newspapers. If a worker wants to join the library he has to go through a lot of red tape imposed by administration in order to get permission.
>
> St Augustine in the true management spirit, have kept the workers divided and exploited, with a blatant disregard for their rights. Workers can only get rights when they fight for it.[11]

The administration was always seen as the enemy in these types of struggles. It symbolized the power structure or establishment as articulated in much of the left-leaning radical ideology of the era. In fact, this division of the power structure and the exploited was simplistic. The university's administration, the political administration, the multinational corporations, and the covert intelligence and security agencies were seen as the established power structure pitted against the workers, radical intellectuals and the students. Lending support to the cause of the workers was one of the ways the Guild council felt it could be meaningful and continue in the vein of 1970. In 1977, another strike by non-academic staff members at St Augustine was supported by some students, but there is no evidence of formal support by the Guild council in the records. Another strike by unionized non-academic staff members in 1980 at St Augustine became destructive, when approximately seventy students invaded the office of the campus principal Lloyd Braithwaite, ransacking furniture and administrative material.[12] Daaga Hall was destroyed by fire during this strike and the administration and the union blamed each other for the incident. Douglas Hall explained, "Students complained that conditions in the library, the cafeteria, and the halls of residence had long been deteriorating, and that lecturers sometimes failed to hold classes."[13] It is unclear whether the Guild had any direct role in these incidents given the scale of the events. The 1977 strike saw the shutdown of the campus for several weeks. The concerns of the students and those of the non-academic staff members were linked by the perception that the university's administration was erecting barriers to block change and progress.

Students on Committees

One noticeable aspect of university affairs from 1973 onwards was the attempt at involving students at the administrative and policy-making level. As a consequence, students were appointed to various university committees that decided policy. Ordinance 18 in the university's charter did make provision for student representation on university committees. In the early 1970s, the Cave Hill and Mona campuses were expanding student representation and restructuring the student/administration relationship expressed through the student Guilds. In the years prior to 1973, this type of involvement was not evident. One reason may be that the Guild was not very vocal in the years

1962 to 1968 and there were no radical confrontations to destabilize the established structure. Between 1968 and 1973, radical activity awoke the administration to the diverse concerns of the student body. After 1973, the UWI administration recognized the importance of involvement and made active efforts to have students represented on committees. The Guild played an important role in this through nomination or election, though members of the Guild's executive did not necessarily sit on committees.

One noticeable effect of this policy of encouraging student involvement, which owed its origin to student radicalism, was the reduction of student/administration confrontation over particular concerns. Including students in the shaping of university policy helped to address the communication gap, though confrontation continued to be an option for bargaining. The students who felt marginalized always voiced their concern, doing so in radical language or in terms of a radical philosophy. But there was some difficulty in using this style by the mid-to late 1970s.

In October 1974, assistant registrar W.S. Chalmers sent letters requesting the faculty representatives on the Guild council to arrange for one student to be elected to the Campus Academic Board.[14] This was the first letter of its kind encountered in the records. In April 1975, with a new Guild council in place, secretary H. Gibson sent out more requests to the president of the Guild, Godfrey Martin, for nominations of student representatives for the Academic Board, Finance Committee, Planning and Estimate Committee, Joint Consultative Committee, Bookshop Committee, Library Committee, Student Affairs Committee, Halls of Residence Committee, Open Lectures Committee, Extra Mural Advisory Committee, Committee on Decentralization, Placement Board, Building and Grounds Committee, Cafeteria Committee, Swimming Pool Committee, and Advisory Committee on Sport, a total of seventeen committees with over two dozen student representatives.[15] Further to this, throughout the 1970s new committees were set up and students were requested to sit on them. For example, in January 1978, Chalmers, now senior assistant registrar, requested student appointments be made to the Appointment (Placements) Board and the newly established Campus Examinations Committees.[16] As stated, the Guild was closely involved in the coordination of this representation either through nominations or elections. As new Guild councils were elected, they were advised by administration to send students to committees as representatives.

Other Concerns of the Guild

As noted earlier, constitutional reform seemed less of a concern in this period and mention of it was absent from many of the primary records being generated; a few articles stated that the existing constitution seemed to have worked well. But, aside from radical activity, the Guild had other concerns.

Among the events featured on the Guild's calendar were sporting activities, such as the Inter-Campus Games. The campus had been a site for sporting activity since its ICTA days, and the spirit had continued unabated. In 1974, the Inter-Campus Games were held at the Cave Hill campus in Barbados. The contingent from St Augustine sent teams for football, basketball, netball, cricket, lawn tennis and athletics. The ICC of the Guild of Students usually benefited from these events because of the regional collaboration they afforded.

Another development in this period was the development of UWI's steelpan group, Birdsong. As stated in a memorandum by Vernon Brewster, the director of Student Advisory Services, to Hugh Gibson, Birdsong was formed as a collaborative effort between the Steelband Club and employees of the university.[17] The establishment of the group in August 1973, which represented Trinidad and Tobago's culture on the campus and off it, was long awaited and the Guild provided significant financial support. An inaugural ceremony was held on 22 September 1973 and the list of invited guests included Gordon Rohlehr, Spree Simon, Bertie Marshall, Lennox Pierre, Ray Holman, Pan Trinbago and J.D. Elder. Birdsong served to link the university with the wider society as many of the band's members were external to UWI. The group also participated in the annual Carnival celebrations, which became a cause for concern as the initial vision for the group's establishment was to have a steel orchestra composed of UWI students.

Another concern about the group was that in its initial stages it was costly. Though the inaugural ceremony cost approximately TT$$500, the group's 1974 carnival participation cost close to TT$$18,000, with a sizeable portion of this expended on operational costs. This effectively placed the Guild in the red by approximately TT$$10,000. Costs remained high as the band played at many events. The administration contemplated taking action to reform Birdsong, which provoked an outcry because many felt that the administration's stance regarding the group was too harsh. In August 1975, Ian Belgrave, president of Birdsong, made the following statement:

> The new students' council that came into office last February has since then shown clearly its design in allegiance with the university Administration not only to severe [sic] all links with the outside community, but to dissociate itself from any link whatsoever with the steelband movement.
>
> Their anti-steelband policy as concerns our band has been in evidence in discussions with officers of the student Guild who openly state (i) that birdsong has become too big for the University and should be cut down (ii) that birdsong includes too many "outsiders" (i.e. non-students) and should be brought back to a "students-only" organization (iii) that students waste too much time beating pan and associating with "undesirables".[18]

The "undesirables" mentioned by Belgrave in his letter presented a great security concern to the campus. While documentary evidence was not found of any breach of security due to the group, the entrance of non-UWI students was unacceptable to the administration. Birdsong eventually was removed from the campus, which saddened many, but cultural activities remained a vibrant feature of campus life.

Orientation was also a great period of activity for the Guild. New students entering UWI had opportunities to familiarize themselves with campus activities, including the many events put on by the Guild of Students. "Grubs", as they were still called in the 1970s, usually underwent an initiation, though later in the decade this became less of a feature for the general student body than for those entering the halls of residence. The *Freshman's Guide* produced by the Student Services usually introduced students to activities on campus as well as the structure of the Guild of Students. It highlighted the upcoming events, the role and responsibility of students, and avenues for participating in student life. Introductions like these would likely have empowered students, allowing them to know about the university and make choices about whether or not to engage in the available activities.

Conclusion

Overall, national and internal circumstances at UWI in the mid- to late 1970s transformed the way the student body and the Guild council operated. Tradition ebbed, superseded as it was by new forms and new types of consciousness. There were radical students, apathetic students, those conscious of culture, those academically inclined and those occupationally inclined. This variety shaped the next decade as it brought a range of issues to the fore among the student body, and the rise of ethnic conflict became a pervasive feature. As one era wrapped up, another one had begun.

Chapter 4

Societal Division Abounds, 1980–1989

The Guild of the 1980s made some departures from that of the prior two decades. If the 1960s marked its origins and the 1970s marked its period of radicalism, the Guild of the 1980s saw a return to normalcy, which laid the foundation for further change. There was continuity, particularly in areas of student apathy, student expression and Guild activities. However, change was also a prominent feature. The decade was characterized by major ethnic and national confrontations among students, internal conflicts and greater expressions of international, regional and national awareness. It could be said that this phase heralded the modern era of the Guild of Students.

Ethnic Confrontation

Throughout the 1980s, the Guild council experienced ethnic conflicts. Guild elections and the creation of Indian and African cultural groups helped fan the flames of conflict in the period and brought the ethnic issue into the open. There was increased attention to the ethnic composition of the Guild council, which had previously been predominantly African. In this regard, the situation on campus mimicked the national scene, where the People's National Movement (PNM), a predominantly African-based party, had remained in power for thirty years.

In the May 1985 issue of *Fusion*, a magazine produced by the Guild's publications committee, an election report noted that "the Guild election this year has proven to be the source of endless controversy, some of it genuine and a lot of it facile. The use of racist propaganda on election day was probably the most distasteful incident of the entire election."[1]

The issue of ethnic conflict evoked many opinions on the issue. Wayne Hayde, 1985–87 and 1989 Guild president, opined that there was rising ethnic confrontation in the 1980s. He stated that during the 1970s, the political groups on campus were mainly African dominated. Some conflict therefore surfaced with the creation of SPIC. He noted that some time after, a rival society emerged, the Society for the Promotion of African Culture, which further increased tensions. This conflict seemed to have tainted Guild elections. Hayde felt that this ethnic conflict began to subside by the end of the 1980s. SPIC's membership became more multi-racial and the group went on to make "an invaluable contribution to the campus".[2]

Some of the student publications in the 1980s illuminated the degree of ethnic conflict on campus and its impact on the Guild, such as SPIC's *Indian Campus Review*. One article in this publication stated that many believed that SPIC was "a racial Indian organization":[3]

(i) SPIC represents Indian Racialism and Indian isolationist tendencies on Campus,
(ii) SPIC practices racial discrimination and,
(iii) SPIC represents all Indian viewpoints.[4]

The author claimed that this image was unfounded, noting that "Indian culture was thought of as something inferior and many Indians were made to feel this way".[5] However, it was admitted that the negative image of SPIC may have arisen after a calypso show in 1973 when a group of Indians were offended by some lyrics in a calypso and walked out of an event in the JFK complex. A SPIC publication in the aftermath of the event noted that

> tension ran high on campus all morning. Some Africans were trying sincerely to understand the Indian position, but many others took arrogant positions from the start. They sought out Indians to engage in verbal combat over a walkout over which many Indians were ignorant. (There were a few Indians in the Calypso show the night before.) Over the ensuing weeks, verbal sniping continued, in classrooms, in the library, in the halls and around the campus.[6]

This episode helped to create an image of SPIC that lingered and became more widespread in the 1980s. The *Indian Campus Review* article further noted that "many academic cycles have passed since then, yet this image of SPIC exists and persists. New students coming on campus, Indian or non-Indian, somehow get the notion that SPIC is racial".[7] The author went on to state some of the positive events the society had been involved in and concluded that "the image that others have of SPIC is fictitious and does not exist in reality; the image SPIC has of itself is a positive one based on modernity and pride for our cultural heritage".[8]

Another student submission, "A Wonderful Journey", disagreed with an editorial written in the *Guardian* by Selwyn Ryan which suggested that every creed and race finds an equal place in Trinidad and Tobago. The student argued:

> At the level of student politics, a biased representation appeared. The Guild council contained only African brethren, and while we concede the fact that they can do a very good job for students they understand, these well meaning boys know nothing about half the students on campus and this sector remains the inert class. It is rare to be an Indian practically living in the Guild Office, the "I" room or the Publications room, not because the Indians do not find use for the amenities there, but because they are treated with hostile glares and demon glances whenever they try to use these areas. In fact, they are socially alienated from the hive of Guild activities.[9]

The issue of the "I" room, a recreation room that was populated by opinionated students, created a point of conflict as the room was perceived to be devoted to the promotion of African history and culture. In fact, this room produced the publication *Riteflow*. One of the objectives of *Riteflow* was "to drive home a sense of responsibility to the Caribbean people about Africa".[10] In addressing the Indian population, the magazine noted, "for our Indian brothers and sisters here in Trinidad the magazine would go a great way to understanding the African man and woman".[11]

Ethnic confrontation became a major campus issue during the 1980s. The conflict engendered a new public discussion that continued after that period. Ultimately, the issue indicated that national societal concerns had begun to penetrate Guild affairs.

Conflict of National Allegiances

During the 1980s, some conflict emerged between students from Trinidad and Tobago and those from other countries, particularly those of the Caribbean. In 1983, the *Undergrad*, an official Guild publication, observed that "faculty, nationality, race, sex and geography"[12] divided students. The observation was made in the light of open conflict emerging; the issue relating to nationality appeared most alarming.

A major issue developed between the students living on the St Augustine campus in what were known popularly as "halls", where mainly foreign or regional students lived, and the wider university student community. In 1983, a conflict occurred between the halls and the Guild council. A writer for the *Undergrad* noted that it was a case of Trinidadians against non-Trinidadians. The halls were accused of scheduling events at the same time as Guild events during Orientation Week and also of not participating in Guild Orientation Week events. Hall members were accused of being unwilling to forge relationships with other campus members. The campus principal in 1988, Professor George Maxwell Richards, noted in a meeting with the Canada Hall committee that there seemed to be "a deteriorating relationship between the general campus community and the residents of Canada Hall".[13] He went on to urge the Canada Hall members to reconcile their differences with other students. It should be noted that Canada Hall residents consisted mainly of Jamaican engineering students. These students had a closely knit culture, which may have affected relations with other students on campus. The changing economic conditions and the increasing challenges of the Caribbean Community at that time perhaps coloured relations among Caribbean people and filtered down into the hall issue. Hall students may also have occasionally felt that the Guild did not treat with their issues. Despite this, it must also be noted that hall students traditionally provided, and continued to provide, major support during significant Guild-led disputes with administration.

Students and Administration: Communication Improves but Conflict Persists

At an official level, communication seemed to be fairly consistent between the Guild council and the UWI administration. Documentary evidence indicates that newly elected Guild councils received an invitation to speak with the university administration. By this time, as we saw, the Guild also coordinated the placement of students on various campus committees. Each new Guild normally received a letter from the university administration asking for representatives to fill various committee positions. These committees included the following:

- Campus Council
- Campus Finance and General Purposes Committee
- Campus Academic Board
- University Council
- Senate
- University Planning and Estimates Committee
- Board for Examinations

The Guild continued to approach the university administration on a number of recurring issues, in which process the relationship with the administration seemed quite strained at times. It appeared, on some occasions, as though the university administration was not quite willing to cooperate and that the students' interests were not always a primary consideration. One editorial in the *Undergrad* described the UWI environment as "drab and depressed", because of "dirty buildings, sparse landscaping and extremely limited students' facilities".[14] The writer expressed boldly that students seemed to be "dogs in the manger when administration sits down to budget and student facilities come on the agenda".[15] It should be noted that this was during the post-boom era in Trinidad and Tobago and therefore a time of financial constraint for the St Augustine campus. The issue of student facilities continued to be a major one throughout the 1980s.

In the midst of such a breakdown in communication, many student demonstrations erupted. In March 1980, the University and Allied Workers' Union, a trade union for support, technical and service staff, declared a strike with some four hundred workers.[16] Months of unsuccessful negotiations between administration and the union had broken down in February 1980 and this subsequently led to the union's decision to strike.[17] One spokesman from the union noted that matters were outstanding since August 1978.[18] The strike severely disrupted the university's services. Meanwhile, the Guild took a lead role in rallying students and representing students' interests. The *Embryo* noted that throughout the issue "the Guild pleaded with the Administration to give the workers what was due to them".[19] They mobilized the students and arranged marches to the administration building. Principal Braithwaite refused to meet with the Guild to attempt to settle the issue, as requested by a crowd of some seventy students, until strike action was stopped.[20] This initiated more marches and protests, again under the leadership of the Guild. On Friday, 18 April 1980, approximately twelve hundred students marched to the administration building, which they found closed.[21] Five hundred students gathered on the following Monday morning and stormed the building; incidentally, this was the tenth anniversary of the State of Emergency that was implemented on 21 April 1970 and marked the beginning of a major standoff.[22]

The principal, who was already under police protection, requested more police officers. Consequently, commissioner of police Randolph Burroughs and his infamous Flying Squad arrived on the campus followed by six buses of police recruits.[23] Students opted to continue occupying the building. Police officers were instructed to clear the building. The situation turned chaotic. Force was used and students began to scamper out of the building. The *Guardian* reported that about fifteen students were injured.[24] The students retreated but efforts at mass demonstrations did not end there. The Guild made attempts to get more students involved as students returned to classes. They made attempts to disrupt lectures, organized demonstrations in Port of Spain and held concerts. Support also came from trade unions and WIGUT, Jamaica. But as examinations approached, the struggle lost momentum. Rifts were created as a result of this turn of events. A number of Guild councillors resigned and, subsequently, the entire Guild resigned and a new, less militant Guild council was installed. This episode marked a peak for student militancy in the 1980s. Mass demonstrations continued during the 1980s, but the nature of these demonstrations was noticeably different from the ones in the decade before.

In 1982, a committee was formed against an increase in fees at the time. The committee, led by the Trinidad and Tobago Students' Movement and supported by the Guild, started a petition that was signed by five hundred students.[25] Later in the year, 150 Canada Hall students conducted a picket demonstration demanding better facilities at the hall. During the demonstration, a group of students met with the principal and were assured their concerns would be addressed. The afternoon of the demonstration some maintenance work was done. Later, in 1987, the main air-conditioning unit in the library experienced some problems and the university administration took a long time to address the issue. According to an article from the Guild's secretarial committee publication *Cote Ci Cote La*, the unit was fixed seven months later. In the meantime, students organized two marches to raise awareness of the issue. Concerns about facilities or services replaced ideology as the motivation for students' mobilization.

Relationship between Students and the Guild

The 1970s for the Guild had been a period marked by radicalism and militancy and that image discouraged some students from participating in the Guild. The 1984–85 Guild president Shiva Sharma made reference to this concern. In his report in the *Undergrad*, it was noted that "the image of the Guild of Undergraduates in the eyes of the general public . . . and students on campus has for years been a very distressing one. Seen as a haven for reactionary, revolutionary or militant groups of students, newcomers to the campus steered away from the institution, having no wish to deal with the supported 'leftist band' that was the Guild".[26] President Wayne Hayde (1985–87 and 1989–90) also highlighted this issue of redefining the Guild away from the image created during the 1970s. He wrote that "in looking at today's students and today's Guild it is clear that the same priority is not placed on political activity".[27] He went even further to describe the Guild of the 1980s as "politically dead".[28]

Some criticisms were directed at the Guild during the 1980s. An editorial published in the December 1982 *Embryo*, produced by the Guild's publications committee, criticized the Guild council's reaction to the many problems facing students. It accused the Guild of showing a "lack of initiative" and noted that "the Guild [was] incompetent to deal with these situations".[29] In the *Embyro* one year later, it was noted that "the current Guild can boast nothing that was done towards alleviating some of the pressure experienced by the student population".[30]

The Guild council received complaints about its alleged lack of responsiveness, willingness and accountability at times. The 14 March 1983 issue of the *Embryo* again criticized the Guild. An incident between students pursuing the Master of Science in accounting and administration went as far as the law courts, and saw a number of students facing possible failure in the course. The Guild was accused of a lack of responsiveness and support in the issue. There was a matter arising with Canada Hall students and the administration with regard to maintenance required at the hall. The Guild was again accused of a lack of willingness to assist these students. *Embryo* noted an alarming lack of accountability, as far as money and records were concerned, at the Guild bar and café. It was also noted that Guild councillors who were sponsored to attend meetings abroad to represent students used the trips for other purposes and failed to produce reports for the meetings.[31] Such criticism indicated some students' perception of the Guild. The Guild had continually to work to foster a good impression of its relevance and effectiveness.

Publications and Student Expression

The 1980s appeared to have been a popular period for publications. A number of publications from the previous decade continued, including *Embyro*, produced by the Guild, and *Riteflow*, produced by opinionated students from the "I" Room. More importantly, the 1980s saw a number of new publications such as *Fusion*, the *Undergrad, Indian Campus Review, Cote Ci Cote La, Students' Voice* and the *Faculty of Arts and General Studies Newsletter*.

Fusion, an official publication of the Guild publications committee, served as an example of the continued efforts to promote student expression on campus. The committee in their 1985 edition noted that "*Fusion* symbolizes an aspiration of togetherness, a blending of the thought, views and ideas of the committed of the University".[32] *Fusion* was simply a manifestation of the publications committee's mandate to be "the mouthpiece of the student population", as well as to "make students aware of all issues that are affecting them as students and other matters that should concern them".[33]

Over the years, there was a commitment to allowing expression of all shades of student opinion. In all the 1980s' publications, articles expressing criticism of the Guild and the university administration were common. Freedom of expression was not restricted. Guild council members were also allowed to address concerns raised through these publications.

Student Apathy

Student apathy continued to be an issue during the 1980s, and it manifested in various ways. Complaints arose regarding students' utilization of the Guild council and its services. One writer for the *Undergrad*, a Guild publication, commented that "there is a tendency to treat elections in a 'jokey' manner".[34] The writer expressed a general view that candidates were nominated on a whim or hastily, the elections fora were trivialized, and students simply voted for friends or attractive candidates. The voter turnout at Guild elections also highlighted the extent of student apathy. In 1983, for example, only 30 per cent of the student population cast votes in the Guild elections.[35]

The Guild council also experienced problems with student involvement in clubs on campus. This qualified as an issue for the Guild council, given its role in supporting and functioning as an umbrella body for student clubs. In the *Undergrad*, "one of the major complaints that [is heard] from students is the absence of clubs on campus".[36] A number of clubs existed only in name and the absence of these clubs contributed to the idea of student apathy. The ICC chairman of 1989 surmised quite bluntly in a report in the *Fusion* that "there are a lot of clubs on campus, some are vibrant and active, others are parasitic scum of the earth".[37]

The Guild council endeavoured to increase students' participation in co-curricular activities. In a 1984 publication, a letter from a student commenting on apathy stated that the word "participation" was heavily mentioned, while it seemed many students were only "interested in the formal academic pursuit on campus".[38] The Guild continued to stress against this reality. In a message to students in 1987, for example, Guild president Wayne Hayde encouraged students to be all-rounders. He noted that students should not "simply be bookworms . . . interaction is also important".[39]

Guild's Contribution to Student Life on Campus

Throughout the 1980s, the Guild council hosted annual orientation programmes and scheduled several cultural, sports and recreational events. Some of these included orientation balls, dinners and panel discussions. There were also sessions involving the Guild council, student clubs and students.

Outside of orientation, there were some occasions where the Guild made itself available to major student fora. For example, in 1987 there was a request by students for a foreign student representative on the Guild council.[40] Representatives from various island associations on campus addressed the Guild council on the issue. While the motion was eventually denied by majority vote, the event showed one example of the Guild's willingness to engage actively with students' concerns.

In reviewing the various 1980s' Guild publications, particularly the addresses from Guild council members, some major emphases are clear. There was a particular focus on student development and there were four major areas that the Guild occasionally gave attention to in its writings. First, there was a focus on developing all-round students. Second, there was a focus on the graduates' impact on society: it was believed that the UWI student should go on to make positive contributions to society. Numerous Guild councils expressed the need for students to begin considering the contribution they could make to society from early in their university career. Third, the Guild council advocated the practical use of knowledge acquired at university. Last, all students were urged to have a proper awareness of student and university issues. As previously mentioned, these concerns were the major reason for the production of the many newsletters and magazines during the period.

Internal Guild Issues

During the 1980s, the Guild council faced a number of challenging internal issues. For example, the entire Guild council (1980–81), with the exception of the president, Philip Ambrose, and the EAC chair, resigned. The president and chair eventually resigned later on and a new Guild council was elected. The implosion of the council was due to a difference of opinion among members over the future course of action in response to a stand-off between the university administration and university staff over wages, which was detailed earlier in the chapter.

The 1983–84 Guild council experienced a conflict among its members over the lack of performance of some councillors. The president of the Guild, Terri-Ann Joseph, the first female president, revealed that some Guild councillors were not performing their assigned duties. She pointed out that some Guild councillors had been forced to take on extra duties to make up for the deficiencies of others. Two Guild councillors in particular were highlighted – the secretary, Sean Douglas, and the EAC chairman, Peter Beddoe. The situation was described as a crisis, as indicated by the public notice released by the Guild calling for a mass meeting on the impasse. As a basis for the meeting it was noted that "unless there [was] an immediate decision by [the two Guild] members to resign the present Guild Council cannot be expected to continue in office".[41]

Throughout the 1980s, numerous problems emerged with the management of Guild elections. This was not unique to this period. Prior to the 1980s election, complaints had arisen about the 1979 election. An article in the *Indian Campus Review* noted a few complaints expressed against "the Returning Officer and the polling agents [who] did not remain impartial [as] some of them were openly calling their friends to vote and frightening off voters from other factions by name calling and other undesirable methods".[42] The article went on to note that this was an allegation and as a result might or might not be true, but it nonetheless called the integrity of the university into question. A report in *Fusion* on the election of May 1985 indicated that the "absence of a well-defined set of procedures created serious problems for the elections and was at the source of many allegations of fraud".[43] These comments highlighted some of the major concerns of students and their perception of the election process.

Though there were allegations of corruption raised against the Guild council, mention of these in the extant 1980s' sources was sparse. An editorial in the March 1983 *Embyro* alleged corruption throughout the previous year. The editorial noted "corruption with Student Guild funds particularly in the Bar and Cafeteria where they abuse the free lunch and drink privileges and at times money is taken from the cash registers by Guild officers without proper procedures".[44] This situation highlighted that corruption was an issue that the Guild council had to address, even if it was only the perception of it.

Party politics seeped, to some extent, into Guild affairs during the 1980s. Some publications during the 1980s provided commentary on the influence of political parties in the Guild and on campus. An editorial in the March 1983 *Embryo* stated that some of the Guild councillors tended to be "young PNMites trained in PNM styled politics in the various PNM youth leagues throughout the country".[45] This was an interesting observation given that the

PNM dominated the national political realm for thirty years. Similarly, in the 1986–87 Guild, there were two councillors, vice-president Roodal Moonilal and EAC chairman Dennis Brown, who were self-proclaimed members of the National Alliance for Reconstruction.[46] The issue of the influence of political parties became more salient by the turn of the twenty-first century.

Forming Regional and International Links

International Youth Day in 1982 marked a major point in international youth collaboration for the Guild. Student organizations from across the Caribbean and Latin America met at UWI, St Augustine, on this day. The conference engaged in discussion on the formation of a Caribbean Union of Tertiary Students.

One of the major regional issues in the Caribbean during the early 1980s was the Grenada Revolution of 1979. During the orientation sessions in the early 1980s, a number of panel discussions were held that focused on the issue of Grenada (for example, "Intervention: An Attack on the Rights of the People – Truth of Grenada").[47] The Guild also organized a mass demonstration with the intention of expressing solidarity with the people of Grenada at a time when the latter were experiencing anarchy and violence. A human ring was formed in an open area near the JFK Auditorium. A year later, in March 1984, the Grenadian Students' Association held a march again to stand with the people of Grenada during a period of trial.

South African apartheid also surfaced as a prominent issue during the 1980s and as a theme for Guild activity. In the 1987 Arts Week, organized by a Guild councillor, there was a specific focus on apartheid in South Africa. The event sought to highlight and show solidarity for "the struggle of [the] brothers and sisters in South Africa".[48] As part of the week, a concert was held that involved African dances, songs and a performance by a band of African drummers to illustrate the South African theme.

The late 1980s marked a core period for greater collaboration between the UWI Guild councils. In November 1987, the first regional Guild council meeting was scheduled to occur using the UWI Distance Teaching Experiment system. This system involved "using satellite and other sophisticated telecommunications techniques to beam classroom, laboratory or other teaching scenes".[49] It could be considered one of the early modes of speedier and more convenient communication between the UWI campuses in the region.

These numerous initiatives by the Guild council showed its continued commitment to greater regional and international collaboration. The student-participation focus of many of these initiatives also assisted in the promotion of greater awareness of regional and international issues.

Constitutional Reform

The issue of constitutional reform remained a concern throughout the history of the Guild. Significant efforts at reforming aspects of the constitution to suit the needs of the St Augustine campus and to reflect current conditions were undertaken.

One of the main concerns regarding reform in the 1980s centred on the annual Guild elections. The Guild elections, as noted previously, were marred by reports of mismanagement and tampering. This led to requests for a more heavily supervised elections procedure.

During the 1980–81 Guild council, it appeared that the Guild constitution came under serious question. A report from the UWI Academic Committee in December 1980 noted that Principal Braithwaite made it known that "there was some controversy over the recent election of the President of the Guild of Undergraduates, St Augustine, arising out of the fact that the Guild had no constitution nor written authoritative direction on the period of office of the President".[50] In a letter sent to Guild president Francis Warner, the UAC secretary at Mona, Jamaica, advised him to begin urgently drafting a constitution for submission to the committee by April 1981.[51] The UWI Finance Committee also at the time expressed concern that no Guild constitution had been registered with the committee.

The drafting of this constitution involved an extensive process. The Constitution Drafting Committee was established by the Guild. Throughout the process, the committee held talks with the principal and the deputy principal. They also took the completed constitution to the student body, which approved it in a referendum held specifically for the constitution. This constitution consisted of a number of changes, including provisions for by-laws, and a finance assessment committee was established. The committee was created to monitor the financial business of the Guild and conduct an internal assessment of the expenditure of Guild funds independent of the UWI auditors.[52] These were some of the changes made. The constitution was submitted to the St Augustine Planning and Estimates Committee in February 1981. Members of that committee and the Guild Constitution Drafting Committee along with other prominent persons were invited to engage in discussion on the constitution.[53] At this meeting, concerns were raised and amendments were also agreed upon. For one, there was a stipulation that postgraduate students and academic staff members of the Finance Assessment Committee be selected from the Department of Management Studies. However, it was pointed out that there might be cases where persons qualified in financial management were found in other departments. The committee, therefore, recommended the word "normally" be inserted in the clause to ensure that qualified persons from outside the Department of Management Studies could also be considered. The issue of persons who were members of Guild students' clubs but not members of the Guild was also discussed. It was agreed that a clause would be added restricting the number of associate or honorary members of Guild clubs. The committee also pointed out a flaw in the constitution in that no mention had been made as to eligibility for membership of the Guild council and for being an elector. The committee agreed on a clause noting only full members of the Guild could become members of the Guild council and vote in elections. The UWI Academic Committee considered the submitted constitution on 18 February 1981 and the UWI Planning and Estimates Committee did so the day after. Both committees approved the new constitution.

Conclusion

Societal divisions among students in the university marked the years from 1980 to 1989. Ethnic confrontation occurred openly and was most alarming during Guild elections. There was also division between Trinidadian and non-Trinidadian students. The period was marked by some other noteworthy features as well. There seemed to be greater attention given to international and regional issues, including South African apartheid and the Grenada Revolution. Some influence from party politics was also evident in the Guild. These issues would continue into the 1990s.

Chapter 5

The Continued Growth of the Guild, 1990–1999

The 1990s marked a noticeable change in the nature of the Guild and Guild activities, with an apparent focus on building the Guild's institutions. Structures were revamped and some physical changes made, and there was a general absence of mass demonstrations, compared to previous periods. Most importantly, there was a major focus on student development: there was a shift away from philosophical issues and activism to student national awareness, student issues and institutional building.

The Guild's Contribution to Student Life on Campus

The Guild continued to emphasize student participation throughout the 1990s, and many activities were organized to encourage this. One prominent activity of the Guild during the 1990s was debating. In 1989, the annual Caribbean Inter-Collegiate Debating Competition was established and was held in various territories across the region each year. Moreover, the Debating Society organized and sent teams from the St Augustine campus, which the Guild council and Student Advisory Services supported financially each year throughout the 1990s. In 1997, the Guild also took the initiative of establishing the UWI National Debating Competition with assistance from senior assistant registrar Victor Cowan. National companies were approached for their participation in the competition. Teams of four employees from each company were asked to enter the competition. The Guild also helped two cross-campus debating teams participate in the Fifteenth Annual World Universities Debating Championship at Princeton University in December 1994.

Throughout the 1990s, the Guild hosted a number of events that touched on national affairs. On 22 March 1994, it invited Basdeo Panday, then leader of the opposition, to hold a session with staff and students, during which they were allowed to ask questions on matters of national interest. This was an attempt by the Guild to make students more nationally aware and interested. In the same year, the Guild council reached out to regional leaders. President Ansil Morris sent a letter to P.J. Patterson, then prime minister of Jamaica, requesting the UWI be placed on the agenda for the next Caribbean Community (CARICOM) Heads of Government meeting. He also requested support in sending one of the three UWI Guild presidents to make a presentation to the regional Heads of Government "stating the views and recommendations for the development of the University from a student perspective".[1] The documents do not show the results of this effort.

The Guild highlighted the issue of racism in a forum it hosted on 23 September 1996. Following the forum, the Guild made a request for the suspension of classes to allow a unity march against racism to be by involving students and staff on 3 October 1996. The purpose of the rally was for the Guild to present its official position on racial discrimination. The principal was also invited to present the university's position on that issue. Principal Compton Bourne noted that he "personally sympathize[d] with the ideals which motivate the Unity March".[2] However, he rejected the request as he felt students and staff should be free to participate or not, depending on their own beliefs or practices.

In 1999, a series of events were organized in collaboration with people external to the university. A panel discussion titled "The Recent Local Government Elections and Implications for Political Parties" was held on 29 July 1999, organized by National Affairs Committee chairman Calvin James. Dr Hamid Ghany, representatives from the United National Congress, the PNM, the Guild of Students and the general public were invited as panellists. Later that year, the Guild also launched the Evolution Series, a three-part conference in collaboration with the United Nations Geoguthic Movement, a Trinidad and Tobago youth organization, to encourage young people to be more involved in developing themselves and the nation. International Youth Day in 1999 was also marked by a week of talks, rallies, cultural and leisure activities as well as further efforts to establish a national student union.

Requests for student parties during the 1990s occurred frequently, as seen in the records of communications between administration and the Guild. Almost every island association and student hall asked to use university facilities to host parties, in addition to the parties officially organized by the Guild. The frequent parties resulted in complaints about their ill effects. For example, the campus relations coordinator forwarded a letter to president Ansil Morris and the administration about a fête held by Canada Hall that disturbed the peace. The fête apparently continued until four o'clock in the morning, which was an hour after the approved cut-off time.

The issue of security emerged as a major problem for the Guild in the 1990s. One student in a letter to the editor of the *Socialite* magazine noted that security on campus was an "inefficient service".[3] He complained that too much attention was paid to the library and not enough to the protection of property such as cars and of persons after dark on campus. However, he was happy about the impact the 1990 attempted coup seemed to have had on campus, since apparently, there was a noticeable increase in foot patrols.

The Guild made numerous efforts to address the security issue. It pursued a healthy relationship with the UWI police, which in 1990 consisted of a staff of thirty-six officers.[4] An article in the October 1990 *Fusion* gave some insight into communication between UWI police and the Guild. The EAC chairman, Clarence Rambharath, met with Superintendent Hugh Roberts, who was head of UWI police at the time. The impression was given that the Guild and the UWI police were willing to work with each other. The 1991–92 Guild council continued to press the security issue. It made attempts to raise the awareness of students, administration and the general public on the various security issues on the campus. In April 1992, a number of press conferences and public discussions were held on security. Following these activities, a Guild report noted that "the University hired more external security and revamped their internal arrangements to improve the safety of the student body".[5]

The Guild council also endeavoured to expose students to regional and international issues. To this end, greater strides towards the formation of regional and international links were made during the 1990s. The 1991–92 Guild council placed its function within a regional perspective and embraced the theme "Caribbean Leadership in Training", in an attempt to encourage "the students and University Administration to place top priority on their respective roles in developing the future leaders of the CARICOM region".[6] Regional meetings of the three UWI Guilds became well established during the 1990s. Official dates were set and arranged yearly at alternating campuses. The Guilds were working more in tandem with each other and reports from the different Guilds were heavily circulated across all three campuses, while communication between the councils also seemed to be heightened in this period.

Together with the guilds at Cave Hill and Mona and the Jamaican Union of Tertiary Students, the St Augustine Guild was represented at the Special Congress of the International Union of Students (IUS) held in Czechoslovakia in March 1991. The team sponsored several amendments to the IUS constitution and a number of them were successful. One main proposal that was accepted referred to the "recognition of the University Guilds as special entities to be given particular consideration in the constitution, including special status as organizations and guaranteed representation on the Governing Secretariat of IUS".[7] The Guild also had representation at the Sixteenth Annual Congress of the IUS held in Cyprus in January 1992. At this congress, the St Augustine Guild secured a place on the Auditing Committee of the IUS, which oversaw the financial affairs of the organization.

The Guild of Students in 1994 was responsible for organizing a visit of international scholars to the campus for a forum along with Dr Junor Barnes, then head of the Department of Biochemistry. The visit involved delegates to a biochemical International Symposium on Second Messenger Systems. (Second Messenger Systems refer to molecules that relay signals from the surface of a cell to molecules inside a cell.) The forum was hosted at the JFK Lecture Theatre and delegates came from the Open University, United Kingdom; Karolinska Institute, Sweden; and the University of Saskatchewan, Canada. The Guild hoped that this could lead to further international contact with current scholarship abroad. In a report it was noted that "with the new contacts obtained through the foreign visitors and Dr Barnes, the Students Guild does intend to keep abreast with all information leading to students scholarship".[8]

The Guild council continued to produce, and support students in producing, publications. However, the publications available during the 1990s were considerably fewer than in previous decades. In fact, there were periods for which no publications could be found. The Guild president for the 1992–93 academic year, in his end-of-year report, writes "for the first time in a number of years we returned to a regular Guild publication in the form of the newspaper, 'The Reporter' ".[9] The publications committee chairperson in this same report notes that this publication was the first of its kind in seven years.[10] Some more familiar publications also continued production in the 1990s. The *Socialite*, a publication from the Faculty of Social Sciences Guild representative, which has been noted in previous chapters, continued to be produced during the early 1990s. The same was the case with *Fusion. Arts in Motion*, a publication of the Faculty of Arts and General Studies representative, was also produced. Publications during the latter half of the 1990s have been difficult to source. This may be an indication of the dwindling production of student publications from the Guild or otherwise. It may also indicate a shift in focus as other activities of the Guild increased. The Guild seemed more interested in engaging students in public events rather than through publications.

Student Apathy

Despite strides in contributing to student life, the Guild still faced the issue of student apathy. It continued, therefore, to give attention to this throughout the 1990s. In this period, the emphasis in combating apathy continued with the slogan "participation is key". In the October 1990 issue of the *Socialite*, a publication by the Guild's Faculty of Social Sciences representative, the following rationale for engaging in extra-curricular activity was given:

> Becoming involved in extra-curricular activities helps you to better understand what you learn in tutorials and lectures. Extra-curricular life on campus makes you understand that the world has enough ordinary intellectuals: Live a little! There's need for some balanced, all-round individuals – So play cricket! Dance! Dramatise! Support Your Guild! – Often those who complain about the "boring life on campus", never lift a finger to become involved. Instead, they live in the library, failing to make a contribution.[11]

One student, describing his first year on campus, noted that "students seemed afraid to participate in the many extra-curricular activities that were held. They were contented to be simply a passive observer".[12]

In this same issue of the *Socialite*, Dennis Brown, former EAC chairman of the Guild, also commented on the "enigma of student inaction", and gave some reasons for it. Noting that "many students of the University of the West Indies have complained of the chronic apathy permeating the life of student participation in extra-curricular activities on campus",[13] he gave two possible reasons for student apathy:

> Firstly, the average age of the student population seems to be lessening every year. One result of this is the fact that the student administrators, the Guild, have to rearrange their annual year-plan to meet the immediate needs of a student population which is becoming more difficult to reach than ever before. Secondly, the average student on campus is beginning to question the very rationale for the existence of the Student's Guild. Ironically, this point is made in light of the fact that the Guild has been increasing its various programmes yearly to meet the objective of making life as comfortable for the students while on campus.[14]

The Arts and General Studies representative, Rejeanne Ramtahal, in 1991 also addressed the issue of student apathy in an issue of *Arts in Motion*. She noted that "participation in extra-curricular activities is fundamental in the growing process, as we must be disciplined, hard-working, co-operative which may require patience and we must be able to manage our time properly. Therefore, I urge you to participate keenly in all activities and programs put forward by the Guild and your faculty. Please offer your services and get involved in UWI activities."[15] In this issue, Ramtahal also further explained why she felt the need to urge students to participate more. She noted that "as a first year student of the Faculty of Arts and General Studies, I am saddened by the apathy exhibited by most of the people in this faculty".[16] She challenged the students' view of the role of historians, linguists, sociologists, poets and dramatists, among others. The article also questioned whether students were aware of the potential contribution of products from the Faculty of Arts and General Studies. She further noted that "at present, the technicians, without a vision, are at the forefront of our society".[17]

Over the years, Guild elections also provided a barometer of the degree of student apathy. Low voter turnouts were regularly noted. One student, describing the 1991 Guild election, noted that

> the spirit of the majority of the student body/electorate . . . boiled down as bhagi. This poor student spirit was reflected in the disappointing turnout at the polls on

election day. The eight hour voting period saw a literal trickle of students into and out of the JFK Auditorium. I don't understand why so many people refused to vote. Did they forget? With all those posters around to remind them I should certainly hope not. They really could have a difference in some of the final tallies.[18]

It should also be noted, however, that by the 1990s, St Augustine had become a commuter campus, that is, a majority of students now lived off-campus. Most students now only spent a few hours on campus, with examination time perhaps being an exception. Perspectives on student apathy in this period must take this significant factor into consideration.

Relationship between Students and Administration

The Guild council continued to perform its function as representative of the students in university affairs. It dedicated time to addressing major issues as well as to improving the relationship between students and the administration.

The issue of fee increases surfaced during the 1990s, a significant one for students. The Guild council embraced their representative role on this issue. The 1991–92 St Augustine Guild council, along with those at Mona and Cave Hill, together rejected proposals from the Committee on Tuition Fees. A protest was staged in November 1991 when students indicated their disapproval of the impending fee increase.[19] Students were simply not willing to pay more fees for what they felt were "poor University services".[20] For example, the 1992–93 Guild council created a committee to engage with the fee increase issue. In their report, they also made it known that this was a regional issue as the two other campus Guilds had also formed committees and were fighting the issue at the UWI board level.

The proposed increase in 1992 did not occur; however, the fee increase came the next year, on 15 September 1993, across all three campuses. President Morris noted that a "nightmare has dawned upon us".[21] He accepted the fee increase but sought to press for improvements for students as a result: "With an increase in fees we must advocate for better conditions on campus and the only way we can do that is by uniting – presenting a force that can effectively tackle the university hierarchy. With the present economic atmosphere of recession prevailing in the Caribbean, it was expected that fees would be increased. However, it is not unrealistic to expect an improvement of facilities here on campus."[22]

Attempts were made by the Guild to bridge the divide between the administration and students. For example, the 1993–94 Guild worked together with the Principal's Office to launch a lunchtime series "designed to develop a sense of student attachment to the University and to a closer relationship between staff and students".[23] One of the events carded was "Rap Session: Principal Talks with Students". This particular event was a direct effort to "develop a closer and more bonding relationship between administration and students".[24]

Relationship between Students and the Guild

Students' perceptions of the Guild played a significant role in the relationship between students and the Guild council. The Guild council was aware of these perceptions, particularly the negative ones, and therefore made attempts to change them. In a 1990 May issue of the *Socialite*, Guild president Sheldon Poujade observed that "there are those who through ignorance of [the] facts would dispute the relevance of the Guild's existence".[25] He continued by noting that "before we ally ourselves with the advocates of 'lip service' marginalized to playing the roles of critics, by opportunity and not by intelligence, let us as individuals seek first the facts before drawing the conclusion".[26] Poujade finished his address by challenging students to come to the Guild with all queries, problems and suggestions.

This view was repeated in the 1990 October *Socialite*, where the EAC chair commented that "the Guild is often accused of doing nothing for students".[27] He went on to point out that "this opinion, espoused by the ignorant among us, is fueled by a lack of information about Guild activities".[28] Similarly, another article in the 1991 *Fusion* commented on this negative perception: "Over the years students at the St Augustine Campus have become increasingly unaware and less concerned about the Student's Guild. Many complain that they are not getting any service from the Guild and as such are dissatisfied with the returns they get on their Guild fees."[29]

The comment on the Guild fees seemed to have significant support among the student population, as the Guild from time to time saw the need to make specific mention of it. President Morris, for example, remarked in an address: "Do not come to the Guild office and tell me that you're not getting your $120 worth."[30] The pervasiveness of this perception encouraged the Guild to continually publicize the roles and duties of the Guild, as well as provide information on expenditures and justifications of those expenditures. President Morris continued by noting that "the Guild subsidizes the gym, lawn tennis courts and the swimming pool in order to enable free access to these facilities".[31] He went on to encourage students to fully utilize those facilities. In the same 1991 *Fusion* article mentioned above, Anil Singh also sought to explain the duties of the Guild, pointing out the Guild council's representation on various university committees, faculty boards, as well as its umbrella and funding role for all clubs and societies, its managing of the cafeteria and pub, collaboration with other Guilds, and funding for various fêtes and concerts.[32]

Institutional Development

The 1990s was a period of infrastructural and internal development for the Guild, and emphasis was placed on efficiently managing the operations of the Guild office. First, there was technological improvement, with the purchase and installation of a computer in the Guild office to improve efficiency and record keeping.

Operations in the bar and cafeteria were also computerized. The Guild saw this as necessary to encourage greater efficiency, productivity and accountability. In fact, with the new computerized system came a new accounting system that was operated in parallel with manual accounts.[33]

The popular shuttle service enjoyed today was started in the 1992–93 academic year, with the Guild playing a role in this service's establishment. In a 1993 annual report, the Guild noted that "a shuttle service was also provided to drop students to their homes around the perimeter of the campus, thereby ensuring that students were as safe as possible during [the exam] period when there is an increase in crime. All this was done with the help of the police on campus and at the Guild's own cost."[34]

An attempt was made to streamline the relationship between the Guild and the campus clubs. Inter-Clubs Committee meetings were regularized and an official list of contacts created.[35] A room was also built to accommodate club meetings and allow for the storage of club items.

Internal Guild Issues

In March 1994, a situation emerged when Guild elections were not held as scheduled. Guild member Elton Wickham wrote a letter to the president and other major university administration officials. Wickham, who successfully contested the post for Guild president in the eventual election, suggested that that "holding elections at this stage [was an attempt] to exclude a large section of the student population, since Elections [were] now destined to be held mere weeks before examinations and after the Semester break".[36] Two days after this strongly worded letter was sent out, the president informed the administration of the election date and the date of inauguration of the newly elected Guild council. Wickham succeeded President Morris, but his accession did not go smoothly. One week after Wickham was elected, the previous Guild delayed preparations for a transfer of power. Hence, Wickham once again wrote a letter to the administration, this time specifically to Principal Richards. Though Morris was, constitutionally, no longer a representative of the students, he was present in Barbados for the regional Guild council meeting. Morris responded by noting that he was still Guild president until 7 May and as such was still able to represent the student body, which he felt was his constitutional right. Furthermore, Wickham was also forced to bring the issue of changing the signatories for the Guild bank account to the principal. Normally, the old and new Guild councils oversaw the change of signatories. On this occasion, there was once again a delay and the principal was asked to step in and inform the bank.

Interestingly, the principal also received a letter in which Wickham tendered his resignation at the beginning of his first semester in office. The letter was seemingly a hoax but the reason that the letter surfaced was revealed a day later, when the principal received a letter from a number of students expressing concern over Wickham. They noted that he portrayed himself as representing undergraduate student interests while he was only representing his own. They noted as an example "the purchase of a minibus, which he has labelled 'his bus' and which he uses for his personal affairs".[37] The principal was asked to intercede to keep Wickham in check. Evidence of clear problems with the Guild president continued to surface. The Guild vice-president at the time, Dionne Ligoure, also sent a letter to the principal highlighting a number of problems regarding the Guild president. She accused Wickham of having a dictatorial attitude and of numerous constitutional infractions. She noted that on a number of occasions financial purchases were made which the Guild council was unaware of; she also wrote of the unconstitutional suspension of the vice-president and possible embezzlement of money.[38]

Perceptions on the Attempted Coup d'État

The 1990–91 academic year began on the heels of a major national disturbance: the attempted coup. Students faced the new semester under curfew conditions. The Guild had to adapt to these conditions and perform services to students in these unique circumstances. One Guild member, K. Clarence Rambharath, speaking about publishing the 1990 edition of *Fusion*, noted that it had to be produced with less available time.

The coup certainly had an impact on student expression. In one letter sent to the editor of the *Socialite* in October 1990, the severe negative impact that many predicted would result from the coup was discussed. The writer noted that a "pseudo-economic crisis" was occurring. The coup was described as having little impact, or as simply highlighting problems that existed well before; many economists had noted that the impact would be short term, and that it was mainly the distributive and not productive sectors that were affected by the events. The writer continued:

> Many businessmen – those who were not looted – were charging exorbitant prices to panic buyers who felt completely threatened by food shortages. TELCO experienced a mini boost in revenue resulting from increased overseas calls as well as local calls. The true victim seemed to be the tourism industry. . . . Many are of the opinion that BWIA was hard hit and lost a lot of revenue when in fact BWIA was incurring substantial losses long before the attempted coup.[39]

Furthermore, the fluctuating economy in the early 1990s was blamed on "the devaluation of the dollar, the removal of the cost of living allowance, the fifteen per cent Value Added Tax, the Cess [a tax that was implemented on tertiary education] University students must pay, and the lack of proper medication and facilities".[40] The writer also seemed to sympathize with Imam Abu Bakr and the Jamaat al Muslimeen.

The UWI Islamic Society published an official statement about the 27 July events in the October 1990 edition of the *Muslim Students' Voice*:

> The Islamic Society, University of the West Indies, views the actions of the leadership and some of the members of the Jamaat Al Muslimeen on July 27th, 1990, as most regrettable, unfortunate and self-defeating. While the Islamic Society does share the view that positive social change is sorely needed in our Republic, we do not subscribe to the type of methodology employed by certain members of the Jamaat to ostensibly achieve this desired end.[41]

As a major national event, the attempted coup did not pass unnoticed on the St Augustine campus. It evoked mixed views and had a short-term impact on student activity.

Conclusion

Student development attained significant importance during the 1990s and the Guild council pursued numerous activities to promote it. The Guild's attention to student development stretched beyond the university, as some of its activities targeted students nationally and regionally. During this activity-rich period, the Guild council continued to face familiar issues of student apathy, internal disputes and its image. However, its active agenda opened the door for the growth of the Guild councils of the next decade.

Chapter 6

Conflict and Development, 2000–2011

The years 2000 to 2011 were a particularly busy period for the Guild council. It made strides in forging greater regional and international links, and other initiatives were successfully pursued with the aim of enhancing student life on campus. But this period was also one of conflict, and the Guild council was in the university and national spotlight on numerous occasions. Election irregularities, for example, marred its history during the 2000s. Some of these conflicts were referred to the national law courts. It also appeared that political parties were involved in Guild affairs, which may have added to the increased activity and excitement. The Guild had to work towards improving its image in order to counter the negative portrayals.

Internal Guild Issues

The 2000–2011 period saw various points of conflict develop. Issues arose around alleged impropriety by Guild members, election irregularities and the academic standards expected of Guild councillors. These conflicts frequently placed the spotlight on the Guild at both a university and national level. Newspaper reports about Guild affairs occurred quite frequently in this period.

In 2001, the Guild faced a major issue involving the unprecedented suspension of a Guild president. Shortly after Navindra Ramnanan was elected, he was allegedly involved in the misuse of funds of the Guild. He denied the allegations against him. In his defence, Devesh Maharaj, Ramnanan's attorney, noted that these allegations were "motivated by matters not connected with [Ramnanan's] administration of the Guild but with his attempt to stop the unrestricted spending and misuse of Guild resources".[1] At a Guild council meeting on 4 May 2001, a resolution to suspend the Guild president was proposed and was successfully passed. Later, the issue of recalling the president was also raised. It was agreed that this matter should be dealt with and put to a vote at a later meeting. Ramnanan acquired legal representation, claiming the actions of the Guild were in conflict with its constitution.

On 15 May 2001, another meeting was held for the purpose of holding a vote on the recall of the president.[2] The High Court of Trinidad and Tobago, however, issued an injunction preventing this meeting from occurring.[3] The meeting happened as planned and voting was allowed; however, campus police intervened and seized the ballot boxes, apparently in compliance with the High Court injunction.[4]

The issue remained unsettled until October 2001. During this time, vice-president Michael Alexander acted in the position of president. In October, a meeting with the Guild and the campus deputy principal, principal and registrar was held and and the participants decided to declare the post of president vacant and to hold a by-election immediately.[5] Ramnanan ran again in the by-election for the position of president, but lost to Katija Khan, the 2000–2001 Guild president, who served the remainder of the term.

The Guild of the twenty-first century faced numerous issues regarding election irregularities. Sometimes recounts were deemed necessary and on other occasions, legal representation was sought and the courts intervened. It could be said that Guild elections gained greater hype and excitement in this period than in any previous decade. The 2001 Guild election provided an extremely close result and was the first case in point. Katija Khan, one of the losing presidential candidates, raised concerns. The returning officer noted that she "expressed in writing her misgivings about the fairness of the elections which . . . may have affected the validity of the elections, a validity which only a recount could remedy".[6] A recount was, therefore, granted. In the recount, Navindra Ramnanan obtained 644 votes and Katija Khan, 640.

After the 2002 Guild election, Danny Maharaj submitted a petition to election officials objecting to the validity of the elections, due to a number of election irregularities. He cited the following as major issues to be addressed:

Breach of Section 37 (i) of the old constitution as concerns the election of a returning officer

Irregularities in the manner of voting, for example: no ink, cases where persons voted twice, inadequate voting list

Date of elections was contrary to the constitutional provision section 37 (v).

The voting procedure affecting Special Voters was flawed

No proper account of ballots

No official seal over the ballot boxes

Security and transportation of the ballot boxes from the voting booths to the UWI voting station

Criteria for persons manning the boxes was flawed.[7]

Maharaj later sought legal advice. His lawyers wrote a letter to then presiding officer Jacob Opadeyi requesting that the publishing of official results be postponed until further inquiries could be conducted. In the end, the results were released and Maharaj lost the election.

In the 2003 election, defeated presidential candidate Maurice Burke outlined "electoral irregularities and slanderous campaigns".[8] Burke, along with residents of various halls, wrote to election officials to alert them about the slanderous campaign being engaged in by Ravi Ratiram, the other presidential candidate. The Elections Committee felt there was an "absence of sufficient evidence [and opted to] advise the candidates in writing to desist".[9] As far as electoral irregularities were concerned, Burke pointed out,

(i) the number of rejected ballots were not made available,
(ii) more persons than required were present at the counting of the ballots,
(iii) there was a mix up with some of the ballot boxes,
(iv) more ballots were for one of the positions, and
(v) no candidates were involved in the ballot counting process.[10]

The elections committee dismissed some of the claims and found difficulty in refuting others. The committee, therefore, concluded that "Given these irregularities, it is recommended that an independent committee be established to look into and determine the validity of these complaints."[11] The newly elected Guild ignored the issue. One newly elected member dismissed the allegations as "sour grapes" on the part of the losing candidates. None of the former Guild council members attended the "passing over" inauguration ceremony, which was unprecedented. The former council members took the lead of their former president Mobafa Baker, who called "the installation of the new Students' Guild a mockery".[12]

The 2005 election was also marked by major disturbances in the election process. Some candidates were initially barred by campus principal Dr Bhoe Tewarie and a recount had to be done. Principal Tewarie barred Fallon Lutchmansingh, Glenn Ramadharsingh and Danny Maharaj, all members of the previous Guild council, from participating in the 2005 Guild elections. This decision was taken after Lutchmansingh revealed serious allegations of financial impropriety regarding Guild funds. The allegation involved TT$$1.8 million unaccounted for due to excessive spending.[13] The matter was taken to the courts where an injunction was granted forcing the university to postpone any election until the matter was resolved. Attorneys for both parties agreed to lifting the injunction and, as a result, the university lifted the ban on the above-mentioned candidates.[14] Former 2003–4 president Ravi Ratiram lodged a complaint about this election when he ran again and lost. This time a formal investigation was launched by the returning officer, Anthony Jackman. Ratiram cited the election records, which revealed 2,298 legitimate votes and 1,925 spoiled ballots.[15] A full ballot recount was done to deal with the concerns. The results remained the same and the new Guild council was installed on 26 April 2005.[16]

Another issue arose regarding the academic standard of students wishing to join and current members of the Guild council. Principal Tewarie commented that "students who fail their examinations want to argue about their 'rights' to run for guild office and to hold guild office. This brazenness from students who wish to 'lead' the student body but cannot even summon the basic discipline required to be a student in good standing I find objectionable."[17] Glenn Ramadharsingh, 1999–2000 and 2004–5 Guild president, also recognized this concern and called for "clearly define[d] . . . acceptable academic standards for candidates [of Guild elections]".[18] This issue, among others, helped to increase support for constitutional reform.

Constitutional Reform

Constitutional reform once again emerged as a pressing issue during the 2000s. The many problems that arose during this period caused many to look to the Guild constitution for possible solutions.

In 2002, Guild council members of the three campuses submitted a code of ethics for Guild council members to the UWI Finance and General Purposes Committee. The code of ethics provided guidance in

- responsibility to duties
- discipline and grievance procedure
- attendance and punctuality
- decorum and dress
- confidentiality[19]

All incoming Guild council members now had to sign the code of ethics. The UWI Finance and General Purposes Committee approved the code of ethics in a meeting on 7 February 2003.

During the academic year 2002–3, a new draft constitution was introduced. This new constitution was used to conduct the April 2003 Guild election. Akins Vidale, former Guild elections candidate, wrote a letter to the campus registrar, William Iton, questioning the validity of the new constitution. He stated in the letter that "It was not until October 2003 . . . that the validity of the document came into question. It was learnt that the ratification process was incomplete."[20] The use of a constitution that was not fully ratified caused some chaos. A by-election was postponed and the Students' Senate, a body consisting of all club or society presidents and selected Guild councillors to oversee Guild matters, was disbanded, among other actions. Vidale noted that "while it was made clear that the new document had not been ratified, the [campus] council decided which clauses it would enforce and which others it would disregard. This situation cannot be allowed to repeat itself. Hence the verification of the document must be done in writing and properly publicized."[21]

The university administration responded by indicating that the new constitution was considered and refined at a campus council meeting in March 2003. Clint Fernandez, then club president of the Debating Society, also enquired about the constitution. Four months after the campus registrar responded to Vidale, the situation had not been settled. Fernandez therefore wrote the following in a letter: "I need not remind you that a number of critical issues revolve around the resolution of this question. Chief among these is the activation and functioning of the Student Senate, which is meant to act as an important check and balance on the Guild Council, and will be entrusted with future reforms or amendments of the Constitution."[22] The acting campus registrar, David Moses, sent another letter to Fernandez four days later, citing the minutes of the same March 2003 meeting.[23]

Two-time president Glenn Ramadharsingh, in 2004, also highlighted the existence of two constitutions and called for the ratification of one of them as the sole constitution to be utilized. He also recommended that a team of former election officials and candidates be formed in order to arrive at a consensus on constitutional reform.[24]

In 2006, the Guild council engaged in another process of reforming the constitution. Fallon Lutchmansingh, the 2005–6 president, felt that "in reviewing the existing document the St Augustine Guild Council thought it necessary to propose the adoption of an entirely new constitution rather than make amendments".[25] The process was described as a long one that involved extensive public consultation. The Guild commented in *Your Guild* that "developing a new constitution is certainly turning out to be a long process. Drafting is in progress but has been delayed . . . due to the need for public consultation and sensitization among the Campus population."[26] On 6 April 2006, the constitution was ratified by a two-thirds majority and sent to the campus council for ratification.

During president Hillan Morean's first term, 2008–9, a constitutional reform process was once again initiated. The aim of the new process was "to improve [the constitution's] clarity and conciseness, as well as to be somewhat standardized with the Constitutions of the Guilds of Students at the Mona and Cave Hill campuses".[27] As constitutionally mandated, the Constitution Committee was created consisting of Shaun A. Reid as chairman, Krystal Mitchell, Khadija Sinanan, Kelvin Cenac and Chevon Knott. Morean, Guild secretary Candace Maharaj and UWI Students Today Alumni Tomorrow president Maurice Burke also assisted the team in thoroughly reviewing and amending the Guild constitution. At the end of this process several changes were made to the constitution. Councillors and committee portfolios were modified to better define responsibilities. New provisions were included involving off-campus affairs, academic affairs and disciplinary committees. Perhaps the most significant amendment was the inclusion of a schedule of election regulations "in order to standardize the conduct of elections".[28] The Guild constitution was officially amended in 2009. This amendment remains the most recent as of 2011.

Relationship between Students and Administration

The Guild during the 2000s made continuous efforts to build a relationship with the university administration, which reciprocated those efforts. The period marked one of generally healthy relations between the Guild and the administration. In spite of this, some conflict did occur, but not in the highly contentious manner that marked previous decades of the Guild's history.

During the 2000s, the Guild council stressed student-centredness in campus activities and university decisions, encouraging the university administration to make decisions with the students primarily in mind. The 2002–3 Guild president Mobafa Baker, on entering office, noted that "the one major change I want to see before I leave office is ensuring that the whole concept of student-centredness stops becoming abstract and becomes a complete reality".[29] The university administration also made attempts to reach out to tudents and increase the focus on student-centredness. The president of the Guild, Katija Khan, was invited by the campus registrar to a meeting to discuss a proposed increase in tuition fees for the 2000–2001 academic year.[30] Here, the university administration engaged the Guild council in the process rather than simply imposing the fees upon students. Similarly, in 2001, the Office of the Board of Undergraduate Studies proposed an initiative to provide leadership training to the Guild of Students' executive members across all three campuses. A letter to the directors of Student Services across all campuses noted the following:

> Our experience has shown that the work of Academic Boards and the Board for Undergraduate Studies especially is enhanced when students are able to contribute effectively. Evidence suggests, furthermore, that student representation on University and Campus boards and committees, mandated in the Governance Report, is at times weakened on account of inadequate knowledge of both the issues and the procedures. OBUS [the Office of the Board for Undergraduate Studies] will (a) assist in preparing the undergraduate students for university meetings and (b) brief incoming elected officers of the Guild at the beginning of the electoral cycles.[31]

In April 2004, UWI chancellor Sir George Alleyne took a day to walk around the St Augustine campus. He set out to "gain insight into what [students] really thought of studying at UWI".[32] It was reported that "students . . . gave their candid, spontaneous views, which were all very positive, on the many benefits of a UWI education".[33] Alleyne also met with the Postgraduate Association and the Guild of Students to discuss a range of issues affecting students.

The university administration continued to strive for a student-centred focus and, in so doing, forged greater collaboration with the Guild. In 2005, Vice Chancellor E. Nigel Harris sent a letter to the principals of the St Augustine, Mona and Cave Hill campuses mandating them to meet with the Guild council executives. This was in response to a letter sent to the vice chancellor by the Guild presidents highlighting a number of concerns. The meetings were held over two days in October 2005. In describing the sessions, the Guild noted that "the meetings were very productive and many guarantees were provided to the Guild".[34]

Parking on campus was a major issue for students. The Guild discussed this issue with the university administration on many occasions. In 2005, the statistics stood at 475 student parking spaces while enrolment was 13,600.[35] In this year, while the Guild continued to agitate for increased parking, it lobbied for improvement of the Heart Ease parking area, an unpaved open dirt space. When it rained, driving students encountered a number of problems. In a series of discussions with the university administration, the Guild council was successful in obtaining a promise for the area to be paved by January 2006.[36]

One of the ongoing issues for the Guild over the years has been security on campus. The Guild has occasionally offered safety tips to students on security. A student complaint system called CAHIERS was also established to file criminal incident reports on campus. The issue, however, required collaboration with the university administration. The Guild, as complaints came in, raised the issues and possible solutions to the director of campus security, campus deputy principal and principal. In 2005, some of the major security concerns involved cars being broken into at the Heart Ease parking area and robberies on the peripheries of campus. The director of campus security agreed to establish mobile police units at strategic points throughout the campus, especially during the exam periods, after an appeal was made by the Guild.

During the 2000s, student protests against the administration were not as frequent or vociferous as in previous decades. There were a few occasions where students felt the need to collectively express their concerns. In April 2010, an issue arose between the university administration and academic staff that drove students to engage in mass demonstrations. The administration and the West Indies Group of University Teachers (WIGUT) were engaged in negotiations regarding an expected wage increase. WIGUT was offered a three per cent increase for 2008–11 but expected a double-digit increase. They responded by protesting, organizing boycotts of classes, and threatening to withhold examination papers and results. A *Trinidad Express* article reported on one of WIGUT's activities: "Classes and meetings at the University of the West Indies, St Augustine campus were cancelled as lecturers and academic staff boycotted work to back their demands for a substantial increase in salaries yesterday [10 November 2010]."[37]

The students felt that they were being unfairly punished for an issue that did not really concern them. The Guild, under the leadership of president Hillan Morean, organized a series of responses. Morean expressed his concern over the actions taken by WIGUT and noted that "the Guild does not support the boycott of classes and the lecturers withholding examination questions, deeming the withholding as 'unlawful and unethical' ".[38] Morean threatened to shut down the campus the following week by rallying the students. On 15 November 2010, the Guild led students in a mass demonstration at various points of the campus including the front entrance of the campus principal's office. Principal Clement Sankat invited Guild executive members for discussion on the issue. Morean informed students that he expressed the Guild's willingness to take legal action if the matter was not quickly resolved. The Guild president also began a hunger strike along with the planned protests. As exams neared and lecturers continued to hint at not releasing exam results, Morean's resolve to continue his hunger strike increased. He ended his hunger strike on 18 November 2010 when lecturers confirmed that they would release results. Two weeks later the issue was settled as WIGUT received an additional 2 per cent increase over the previous offer of 3 per cent, which they accepted.

Relationship between Students and the Guild

The image of the Guild was seriously jeopardized as a series of unfortunate situations, including allegations of impropriety, surfaced. There were also questions regarding the effectiveness of the Guild. Many students perceived that Guild council was not doing all it could for students. Denzil Mohammed, a *Trinidad Guardian* columnist and UWI undergraduate student, conducted a short survey in 2003. Students were asked if the Guild needed to do more to involve students. Of the respondents, 85 per cent said "yes" while 15 per cent said "no".[39] This was also made clear in an interview with 2004–5 Guild president Glen Ramadharsingh. Alake Pilgrim noted that "some students at the St Augustine Campus have been challenging the Guild to make positive change in certain areas".[40] To this, Ramadharsingh responded by calling for more detailed accountability for Guild funds, regular public fora to discuss students concerns, and constitutional and electoral reform.[41]

Students expressed some concern with the extent of Guild representation of the students' interests. The 2005–6 vice-president, Keron Niles, criticized the Guild for not effectively being a voice of the students. In an interview, he noted that "as a student it's very plain for me in terms of a voice . . . there is a void on campus in terms of students being mute . . . it's not that the voice isn't there but students feel there is none – the Guild Council has to be that voice".[42]

The low voter turnout at elections also indicated a lack of interest in the Guild by university students. The Guild, in response to this perceived lack of interest, continued to make appeals to the student population to get involved and make use of the Guild.

The Guild sought to build its relationship with students using some of the many initiatives previously mentioned, including the *Your Guild* magazine and public discussions. These initiatives were intended to keep students aware of Guild events and responsibilities. The Guild was aware of the potential harm to its image due to the various allegations and conflicts of this period and saw the need for continuing efforts at improving its image.

The Guild's Contribution to Student Life on Campus

The Guild continued to make strides in enhancing student life on campus. In February 2001, the Guild implemented Campus Carnival in an attempt to mirror the national carnival. It involved a calypso and extempore competition, a fête and parade of bands around the campus. This event would later become an extremely popular and much anticipated annual event of the Guild. Over the years, Campus Carnival continued to grow tremendously. In 2002, the Guild invited other tertiary institutions to the event, including the Hugh

Wooding Law School and John Donaldson Technical Institute. Ten years later, the event continued to grow to such an extent that it became problematic. The 2011 parade of bands and party had over ten thousand persons in attendance, many of them unconnected to UWI, which led to the premature end of the event.[43] In recent years, criminal activities and drunken misbehaviour have become a serious concern at the event. A letter to the editor in the *Express* noted that

> it is a known fact that the administration has had a hard time working with the Guild of Students over the years to contain this matter that has become a serious security nightmare, endangering the lives of not just those who revel in the parade but other students, staff members and residents, in and around the campus. A number of rapes, robberies, stabbings, hand fights and weapon-assisted scuffles have plagued the campus carnival.[44]

In 2012, the administration placed a moratorium on Campus Carnival until more adequate security measures could be put in place.

The Guild has given specific attention to the problem of HIV and AIDS over the years. With knowledge that the Caribbean Basin has the second highest rate of HIV and AIDS in the world, the Guild felt it necessary to engage with the issue.[45] In 2005, an HIV and AIDS awareness campaign was conducted. The administration held an expo in commemoration of World AIDS Day on 1 December 2005, which the Guild's awareness campaign supported. It called for students to wear red on the day and to come out to the event.[46] The Guild has continued over the years to contribute to HIV and AIDS awareness and supports initiatives implemented on campus. For one, it commonly recognizes World AIDS Day in some form each year.

The Guild established the committee Planters for Social Change in the 2007–8 academic year.[47] The committee sought to remedy the problems of high food prices and food scarcity. The erection of a food park at the grounds of the all-female Trinity Hall commenced. The park utilized a variety of growing techniques including container gardening, grow boxes and raised beds for growing a mix of herbs, short-term crops and fruit trees. The park was realized through the collaboration of the Guild council, Trinity Hall administrators, and various departments of the administration including the Office of the Campus Principal and the University Field Station. This Guild initiative highlighted its support for innovation on the St Augustine campus.

In March 2009, the Health Service Unit of the St Augustine campus conducted a survey titled "Alcohol Use Disorder". Of the students surveyed, 70 per cent used alcohol, 20 per cent engaged in binge drinking and 25 per cent engaged in hazardous or harmful drinking behaviours.[48] The Health Service Unit collaborated with the Guild council to address the problem flagged by these statistics. Together, they developed a comprehensive alcohol policy, which was submitted to campus management for consideration.

In efforts to educate and engage students on a number of issues, public lectures and discussions were initiated by the Guild. During two different Guild council terms, there were concentrated attempts to schedule these events frequently. The Guild council established a lecture series in 2005. On 10 November 2005, a lecture titled "Party and Events Planning" was held. Marlon Grant of Island People, an entertainment and events management company, and Casey Cumberbatch of Triniscene, a company dedicated to promoting Trinidad and Tobago's culture, nightlife and entertainment industry, were invited to share their expertise on the lecture's theme. On 24 November 2005, another lecture was held on Zen Buddhism, where a Buddhist monk was invited. While the odd lecture may have taken place after this series, it was not until 2011 under the presidency of Amilcar Sanatan that there was yet another push for a Guild lecture series. This series was entitled Caribbean Reasonings. It sought to consider a number of traditional and modern perspectives on a range of social issues in the Caribbean. The first public lecture was held on 9 June 2011 and featured Donisha Prendergrast, granddaughter of Bob Marley, who covered the Rastafari movement in Trinidad and Tobago. The Caribbean Reasonings lecture series ran for six months and ended on 21 November 2011. During this time, public lectures were held on Hinduism, Christianity, Islam, atheism, the legalization of marijuana, female sexuality, and homosexuality.

The Guild's emphasis on student publications continued to decline. There were significantly fewer Guild and student publications in the 1990s, and in the 2000s, there was further decline. In fact, the university administration stepped in and introduced a consistent campus publication, the *St Augustine News* (*STAN*). This magazine is a prominent university publication that also covers student affairs; it was redesigned and widely circulated from 2002. The Guild council supported this initiative by providing a representative and making occasional contributions. The April–June *STAN* saw an appointed Guild of Students correspondent, Jason Nathu,[49] and his article "The Guild of Students Celebrates 40 Years" was also published in this edition.

Throughout the years, the Guild and student clubs produced some publications that appeared irregularly and often only for short periods of time. One notable publication has been the *Your Guild* magazine, which was created during the 2005–6 Guild council's term, to keep students aware of the Guild's activities and student issues. It was also an attempt to encourage student participation in the Guild's activities. Kieran Khan, the publications committee chair for the 2005–6 academic year, noted that the magazine followed the Guild's "motto to encourage students to 'get involved' ".[50] The magazine, though not always consistent, continues to be produced up to the present day with the 2011–12 edition being revamped for print and online access to students.

Forming Regional and International Links

From 2000 to 2011, there were significant developments in forming regional and international links. The St Augustine campus forged stronger links with the other two campuses and gained greater exposure and recognition internationally. The Guild in this period continued to work toward building and maintaining the strong links established.

The Guild council sent representatives to the Caribbean Federation of Youth Congress's annual general meeting, which was held in St Maarten in June 2001. Wendell Wallace and Mobafa Baker represented the Guild at the congress.

In 2002, Guild council members of the St Augustine, Cave Hill and Mona campuses sought to reach out across the region and establish closer relations among themselves. They proposed the establishment of an inter-campus Guild council:

> The University has over the years seen the importance of "regionalism" and the collaboration of efforts to effect proper decision-making. As such the University has facilitated a cross-campus committee of Deans, Librarians and other special groups to have fora for discussions of their special interest to facilitate effectiveness. The Guild as an institution of the University is no different, in that it has special interests and concerns, which require cross-campus dialogue, collaboration and student

leaders contribution to student learning and development. The recent Student Services Audit from the Board of Undergraduate Studies importantly notes that the quality of student life is different on the three campuses. This proposed intercampus Guild council will facilitate the formulation of best practices for the betterment of governance not only for the Guild but to help to further the University's mission. However, the current situation of Guild Presidents only meeting coincidentally at cross-campus meetings is not an adequate condition to tackle the problems of the Guilds.[51]

This compelling argument made by the Guild councils of the three UWI campuses was favourably considered by the UWI Finance and General Purposes Committee. The principal of Mona commented that the "students should be commended for this initiative".[52] At a meeting on 7 February 2003 of the committee, the proposal was approved.[53]

From 2 to 4 March 2005, the Guild of Students, in collaboration with the administration, hosted the first student Summit of the Americas at the St Augustine campus, titled "Hemispherical Student Summit of the Americas". Students, government agencies and tertiary education providers from various countries gathered to discuss hemispheric issues, particularly those surrounding the establishment of the Free Trade Area of the Americas. The summit sought specifically to bring together stakeholders of the education sector in the Western Hemisphere, explore the impact of the Free Trade Area of the Americas on access to education and quality of education, as well as showcase various universities and student governments through a university expo village.

In the 2005–6 academic year, the Guild organized UWI St Augustine student representation at a number of international events.[54] These included the Sixteenth International Festival of Youth and Students in Caracas, Venezuela; the Harvard Model United Nations debate; and a general visit to Kenya, East Africa.

In 2010, the Guild sought to respond to the severe damage St Lucia and St Vincent and the Grenadines sustained due to Hurricane Tomas. The Guild worked along with the St Vincent and the Grenadines and the St Lucian Students Associations to collect food and supplies to aid the two countries affected. These significant links made by the Guild indicated its adaptation to a period of increasing globalization.

Student Apathy

The issue of student apathy remained a problem that the Guild council faced. One particular area where student apathy continued to surface was that of the Guild elections. One Milner Hall student, in a letter to the editor, commented that as far as elections were concerned the students "seem to have reached a stage of apathy, inaction and unconcern".[55] Denzil Mohammed also addressed the issue. He noted that "students will still vote for their friends, still not ask questions so as not to make anyone feel badly, and will still not get angry because of the long tradition of misinformation and apathy".[56] Mohammed's comments, particularly about the long tradition, can be substantiated in the accounts of the previous decades of the Guild, as seen in the preceding chapters.

The long trend of low voter turnouts at Guild elections continued in the 2000s. In the 2003 election, 2,139 students voted out of a student enrolment of 10,568.[57] This equated to 20.4 per cent of the student population, which was generally the average for the period. The turnout for by-elections has been even lower. In a 2005 by-election for two Guild posts, only 3.7 per cent of the student population voted.[58] Hillan Morean, Guild president from 2008 to 2011, assessed that "normally about 20 percent of the student population comes out to vote every year".[59] He suggested, "It is partly the Guild Council's fault for not reaching out to the students and also the student body themselves who seem disinterested in the guild. The only way to restore confidence in the Guild Council is to address the issues affecting the students and show them results."[60] Morean's comments testified to the continued existence of one of the issues the Guild has had to deal with since its inception.

National Circumstances

There was evidence that national circumstances influenced Guild affairs. Issues such as crime and politics emerged on the campus. These issues, therefore, became Guild issues. Perhaps one of the biggest issues facing Trinidad and Tobago in the first decade of the twenty-first century was crime, where a sharp increase in criminal activity was witnessed. Property crime went from a little under ten thousand cases in 1997 to around fifteen thousand by 2007.[61]

Violent crime jumped from around one thousand cases to well over two thousand cases by 2007.[62] During this time the rate of detection for serious crime stood at only 42 per cent.[63] It was therefore no surprise that crime also significantly affected the St Augustine campus. Guild president Fallon Lutchmansingh made this correlation as she wrote in *Your Guild*: "The St Augustine Campus has not escaped the national reality of the continuous increase in crime. Many cars have been broken into at Heart Ease (student) carpark and students continue to be robbed on the periphery of campus. The most daunting report this semester has to be that of a student being robbed at 12 noon near the north gate on the bus route!"[64] The issue of security, therefore, gained priority on the Guild council's agenda.

National politics continued to infiltrate the Guild council. In the 2005 July–September edition of *STAN*, it was noted that "Over the years, there has . . . been a challenge [regarding] the speculation and accusations, at times, of political affiliation of the Guild of Students."[65] In an interview, the 2005–6 president, Fallon Lutchmansingh, confessed that "post election [we have] been approached by political groups and [we have] had to say that we are apolitical".[66] There have also been allegations of direct influence by political parties on Guild elections. One candidate in the 2008 Guild election made this claim as he protested a decision taken by the Guild. He noted that "previous guild elections have been fraught with allegations of outside political interference"[67] and wondered whether this was the case again in the 2008 election. As further evidence of the influence of political parties on the Guild, it should be noted that several former Guild presidents of this period became national politicians. Glenn Ramadharsingh currently serves as minister of the people and social development and Ravi Ratiram serves as a government senator for the United National Congress. Natasha Grimes unsuccessfully contested the 2010 local government election for the PNM in the Cocoyea/Tarouba region in San Fernando.

Conclusion

The experience of the Guild of Students during the 2000s was one of heightened contrast. There was significant growth and development that helped the Guild council to adapt to the changing environment of the twenty-first century. Great strides were made in the area of student development and in forming strong regional and international links in an era of globalization. The Guild council, at times in collaboration with the university administration, meaningfully improved student services and facilities. In contrast, the conflicts of the period were explosive, which sometimes put a halt to the day-to-day management of the Guild. The media became increasingly attracted to internal Guild issues. The Guild has, however, come a long way since its inception in 1962 and though issues remain, it has the potential to continue moving forward.

Appendix 1

Timeline

1960	Merger of the Imperial College of Tropical Agriculture and the University College of the West Indies; St Augustine becomes the second campus of a regional university
1962	Founding of the University of the West Indies and the Guild of Undergraduates
1965	Draft constitutional reform proposal put forward
1968 (March)	Geddes Granger assumes office as president of the Guild of Students
1968 (October)	March to Port of Spain led by Geddes Granger in support of Guyanese lecturer Walter Rodney and opposition to the ban on his re-entry into Jamaica
1969	Protest over the detention of Caribbean students at the Sir George Williams University in Canada; Granger leads a campus demonstration during an official visit of the governor general of Canada Roland Michener
1970	March to Port of Spain led by Jamaican student Carl Blackwood, president of the Guild of Students; Roman Catholic Cathedral vandalized
1973	Shift in policy to include students on university committees
1973	Some students at Mona support non-academic staff in demonstration for better wages and working conditions; some students at the St Augustine campus lend support to non-academic staff at St Augustine when they strike
1977	Shutdown of the campus when non-academic staff strike with support by some students
1980 (March)	Unionized non-academic staff stage a demonstration for better pay and working conditions with some students in support; students' concerns regarding poor study and recre-

	ational facilities are also voiced; seventy students besiege the Office of the Campus Principal (Lloyd Braithwaite) to highlight concerns; Daaga Hall destroyed by fire
1980	The entire Guild council resigns after a major dispute with the administration and an ongoing strike involving the university and Allied Workers' Union
1981	Submission of Guild of Students constitution to university committees
1985	May election marked by allegations of ethnic clashes
1987	First regional Guild council meeting held over the UWI Distance Teaching Experiment system
1989	Annual inter-collegiate debating competition established with partial involvement from the St Augustine Guild
1991	The Guild councils of the three campuses attend the Special Congress of the International Union of Students (IUS)
1992	The St Augustine Guild is placed on the Auditing Committee of the IUS
1993	The Guild of Students shuttle service begins
1994	Guild election held one month after constitutionally due
1997	The Guild of Students hosts UWI National Debating Competition
2001	Navindra Ramnanan becomes the first Guild president to be suspended
2001	St Augustine Campus Carnival is founded
2002	Mona, Cave Hill and St Augustine Guild councils propose a code of ethics for Guild council members, which is approved in February 2003
2003	Inter-Campus Guild Council is established involving the Mona, Cave Hill and St Augustine Guild councils
2005	Guild of Students in collaboration with St Augustine campus administration hosts first Hemispherical Student Summit of the Americas in March
2011	The Guild of Students hosts Caribbean Reasonings lecture series including eight lectures on Rastafarianism, Christianity, Hinduism, Islam, atheism, the legalization of marijuana, female sexuality, and homosexuality

Appendix 2

Past Presidents of the Guild of Students

1961–62	E.J. Giuseppi (UCWI)
1962–63	Mr Hilbertus A.D. Chesney (British Guiana) (UCWI)
1963–64	Percy N. DeGannes
1964–65	Delf O. King
1965–66	Hollis Charles
1966–67	Anthony Gonzales
1967–68	Wilfred Phillips
1968–69	Geddes Granger
1969–70	Carl Blackwood
1970–71	Colin Edwards
1971–72	Sheridan Gregoire (December 1971 by-election – Keith Smith)
1972–73	Keith Smith
1973–74	Ronald Hinds
1974–75	David Abdullah (November 1974 by-election – Godfrey Martin)
1975–76	Godfrey Martin
1976–77	Keith Joseph (October 1977 by-election – Greg Franco)
1978–79	Liaquat Khan
1979–80	Carl Regis
1980–81	Ambrose Phillip (January 1981 by-election – Frances Warner)
1981–82	Gregory Hernandez
1982–83	Elton Wickham
1983–84	Terri-Ann Joseph
1984–85	Shiva Sharma
1985–86	Wayde Hayde
1986–87	Wayde Hayde

1987–88	Milton Sylvester
1988–89	Milton Sylvester
1989–90	Wayde Hayde
1990–91	Sheldon Poujade
1991–92	Rennie Dumas
1992–93	Kiran Singh
1993–94	Ansil Morris
1994–95	Elton Wickham
1995–96	Kirt St Bernard
1996–97	Marlon Jameson
1997–98	Raymond Leemon
1998–99	Deke Cateau
1999–2000	Glen Ramadarsingh
2000–2001	Katija Khan
2001–2	Navindra Ramnanan (October 2001 by-election – Katija Khan)
2002–3	Mobafa Baker
2003–4	Ravi Ratiram (November 2003 by-election – Arnold Ram)
2004–5	Glen Ramadharsingh
2005–6	Fallon Lutchmansingh
2006–7	Rodney Jaglal
2007–8	Natasha Grimes
2008–9	Hillan Morean
2009–10	Hillan Morean
2010–11	Hillan Morean
2011–12	Amilcar Sanatan
2012–13	Kevin Ramsewak

Appendix 3

Student Numbers, St Augustine Campus

Student	Numbers
1961–62	96
1962–63	146
1963–64	583
1964–65	780
1965–66	910
1966–67	964
1967–68	1,087
1968–69	1,267
1969–70	1,511
1970–71	1,671
1971–72	1,862
1972–73	1,967
1973–74	2,114
1974–75	2,202
1975–76	2,229
1976–78	2,310
1978–79	2,489
1979–80	2,661
1980–81	2,923
1981–82	3,144
1982–83	3,125
1983–84	3,197
1984–85	3,428
1985–86	3,728
1986–87	3,803

Student	Numbers
1987–88	4,156
1988–89	4,209
1989–90	4,147
1990–91	4,137
1991–92	4,529
1992–93	4,947
1993–94	5,191
1994–95	5,231
1995–96	5,321
1996–97	6,007
1997–98	6,303
1998–99	6,634
1999–2000	6,860
2000–2001	6,967
2001–2	7,641
2002–3	8,664
2003–4	10,528
2004–5	11,734
2005–6	13,220
2006–7	15,718*
2007–8	15,824*
2008–9	16,094*
2009–10	15,462*
2010–11	17,636*
2011–12	18,708*

Source: The University of the West Indies Official Statistics, 1999/2000.
*Student statistics, 2010–2011

Notes

CHAPTER 1

1. Bridget Brereton, *From Imperial College to University of the West Indies: A History of the St Augustine Campus, Trinidad and Tobago* (Kingston: Ian Randle, 2011), 63.
2. "Club Reports", *Sundowner*, 1957, 53–59.
3. Ibid., 54.
4. Carlyle B.A. Ross, "Guild Activities", *Sundowner*, 1963, 18.
5. Ibid.
6. Sam St John, editorial, *Augustinian*, 1966, 5.
7. "Your Students' Guild", *Fresher's Guide* (St Augustine, Trinidad and Tobago: University of the West Indies, 1967), 3.
8. Gordon Rae and Christopher Strong, editorial, *Sundowner*, 1962, 3.
9. Editorial, *Sundowner*, 1963, 2.
10. F.V.P. Harvey, "Responsibility", *Sundowner*, 1964, 2.
11. Editorial, *Magnet*, 1967, 1.
12. Guild of Undergraduates, editorial, *Magnet*, 15 March 1968, 1.
13. Canada Hall, "Student Interest in World Affairs", *Canadian*, c. 1967, 3.
14. Guild of Undergraduates, "The Role of the Student in Social and Economic Development", *Augustinian*, c. 1965, 2.
15. Guild of Undergraduates, editorial, *Augustinian*, 1967, 4.
16. "Origin of Opinion", *Opinion*, c. 1961, 2.
17. F.H. Bowen, correspondence to UWI secretary Victor Archer, 13 March 1964 (Student Administration Archive, University of the West Indies, St Augustine, Trinidad and Tobago [hereafter SAA, UWI St Augustine]).
18. Carl E. Jackman, correspondence to UWI secretary Victor Archer, 3 March 1965 (Guild of Students Archive, University of the West Indies, St Augustine, Trinidad and Tobago [hereafter GSA, UWI St Augustine]).
19. Delf O. King, correspondence to senior assistant registrar Arthur E. Burt, 19 March 1965 (SAA, UWI St Augustine).

20. A.L. Armitage, J.Z. Bowers, C. Iverson, H. Leussink, *West Indies: Development of the University of the West Indies, May–June 1968* (Paris: UNESCO, 1968), 124.
21. Brereton, *From Imperial College*, 51–65.
22. Ibid, 59.
23. Guild of Undergraduates, "UWI Student Mission to the Eastern Caribbean" (press release), 12 July 1966.
24. Anthony Gonzales, correspondence to pro vice chancellor, May 1966 (SAA, UWI St Augustine).
25. "Editorial", *Sundowner*, 1960, 2.
26. Guild of Undergraduates, letter to the editor, *Magnet*, 20 October 1967, 2.
27. Ibid.
28. Guild of Undergraduates, letter to the editor, *Magnet*, 17 November 1967, 3.
29. Guild of Undergraduates, "Students of This Campus, Arise", *Magnet*, 15 December 1967, 2.
30. Guild of Undergraduates, *Magnet*, 13 October 1967, 2.

Chapter 2

1. Editorial, *Magnet*, 8 March 1968, 1.
2. "Shearer: Rodney Is a Risk to Jamaica", *Express*, 18 October 1968, 1.
3. Roy Mitchell, "The Making of Makandal Daaga", in *The Black Power Revolution 1970: A Retrospective*, ed. Selwyn Ryan and Taimoon Stewart (St Augustine, Trinidad and Tobago: Institute of Social and Economic Research, University of the West Indies, 1995), 97.
4. Ibid.
5. Ibid., 99.
6. Makandal Daaga, "The Making of 'Seventy'", in *Black Power Revolution*, ed. Ryan and Stewart, 181.
7. Mitchell, "Making of Makandal Daaga", 111.
8. Faye Fraser, "Reflections on the Idea of a West Indian University" (editorial), *Pelican Annual 1968* (St Augustine, Trinidad and Tobago: University of the West Indies, 1968), 3.
9. Pro vice chancellor Dudley Huggins, correspondence to Guild president Geddes Granger, 1 November 1968 (SAA, UWI St Augustine).
10. Brereton, *From Imperial College*, 69.
11. David Murray, *Vanguard*, 21 March 1970, 5.
12. Syl Lowhar, "Black Power in Human Song", in *Black Power Revolution*, ed. Ryan and Stewart, 203.
13. Editorial, *Canadian*, March 1969, 1.

14. Editorial, *Canadian*, February 1970, 3.
15. Brereton, *From Imperial College*, 69.
16. Dave D'Abreau, "Thomas Camacho and Chaos: Reflections on the students revolt at St Augustine", *Vanguard*, 25 October 1969, 6.
17. Ibid, 7.
18. Brereton, *From Imperial College*, 70.
19. "ANR Welcomes 'New Mood' in Youth", *Express*, 27 February 1970, 1.
20. The Editor, "Falling by the Wayside", *Express*, 28 February 1970, 4.
21. The Editor, "And Now to the Constructive Phase", *Guardian*, 11 March 1970, 10.
22. "Guild Accuses Police of Harsh and Brutal Acts", *Express*, 1 March 1970, 3.
23. Winston Gannessingh, "Wanted: A Revolution", *Embryo*, 4 December 1970, 3.
24. "The Future of UWI", *Embryo*, 18 December 1970, 1.
25. Adolfo Gilly, "Dying Colonialism", *Embryo*, 6 November 1970, 2.
26. Surujrattan Rambachan, letter to the editor, *Embryo*, 4 December 1970.
27. Kenneth Parmasad, "Reply to Yusuf Omatunde", *Embryo*, November 1971, 5.
28. "Student Power: Nova Scotia Leads the Way", *Magnet*, 8 November 1968, 4.
29. Bill Riviere, "Liberate", *Insight*, 1974, 36.
30. "A Brother" and "Caribbean Affairs: A View of the Revolution", *Canadian*, November 1970, 5.
31. Topi, "Reflections on the Question of a System Change", *Arts Annual*, ed. Anson Gonzalez, June 1971, 9.
32. Guild president Sheridan Gregoire, correspondence to UWI St Augustine secretary Hugh Gibson, 23 October 1971 (SAA, UWI St Augustine).
33. Ibid.
34. UWI St Augustine secretary Hugh Gibson, correspondence to Guild president Sheridan Gregoire, 22 November 1971 (SAA, UWI St Augustine).
35. UWI St Augustine secretary Hugh Gibson, correspondence to Professor A.R. Carnegie, 17 November 1977 (SAA, UWI St Augustine).

Chapter 3

1. Brereton, *From Imperial College*, 70.
2. "Unity, Imperialism, and Cricket", *Embryo*, 1 February 1973, 5.
3. Rawle Aimey, "Caribbean Economic Problems", *Embryo*, 27 May 1974, 19–20.
4. Cassandra Gopaul, "Elections in Perspective", *Embryo*, 18 March 1976, 7.
5. Editorial, *Students for Change Manifesto*, November 1976, 4.
6. Editorial, *Students for Change Manifesto*, 1976, 5.
7. "Aims and Objectives of Students for Change", *Students for Change Manifesto*, c. 1976, 4.

8. Only one copy of this serial was found.
9. Vernon L. Lawrence, "A Look at UWI", *The Voice of the Hermits*, (St Augustine, Trinidad and Tobago: University of the West Indies), 1.
10. Bro Lasana, "Kaiso Suppressors", *Riteflow*, c. 1979, 9.
11. "The Plight of the Campus Worker", *Embryo*, 3 February 1973, 2.
12. Brereton, *From Imperial College*, 86 – 87.
13. Douglas Hall, *The University of the West Indies: A Quinquagenary Calendar, 1948–1998* (Kingston, Jamaica: The Press, University of the West Indies, 1998), 110–11.
14. Assistant registrar W.S. Chalmers, correspondence to Faculty of Engineering representative, 21 October 1974 (University of the West Indies Archives, University of the West Indies, St Augustine, Trinidad and Tobago [hereafter UWIA, UWI St Augustine]).
15. UWI secretary Hugh Gibson, correspondence to David Abdullah, 15 April 1975 (UWIA, UWI St Augustine).
16. Chalmers, correspondence to Franco, January 1978 (UWIA, UWI St Augustine).
17. Director of Student Advisory Services Vernon Brewster, correspondence to UWI secretary Hugh Gibson, 27 August 1975 (UWIA, UWI St Augustine).
18. President of Birdsong Ian Belgrave, correspondence to President Pantrinbago (Eastern Region), 21 August 1975 (UWIA, UWI St Augustine).

CHAPTER 4

1. "The Guild Elections Report", *Fusion*, May 1985, 17.
2. Wayne Hayde, "A Changing Society", *Fusion*, October 1989, 14.
3. "Image and Self: Images of SPIC on Campus", *Indian Campus Review*, June 1988, 6.
4. Ibid.
5. Ibid.
6. Ibid., 9.
7. Ibid.
8. Ibid., 11.
9. "A Wonderful Journey", *Indian Campus Review*, February 1980, 13.
10. "Riteflow", *Riteflow*, March 1982, 2.
11. Ibid.
12. Editorial, *Undergrad*, November 1983, 1.
13. Minutes of meeting on Canada Hall maintenance, 19 April 1988 (UWIA, UWI St Augustine).
14. Editorial, *Undergrad*, November 1983, 1.
15. Ibid.

16. "21 Years of Students' Struggle for Democracy and Justice", *Embyro*, 14 March 1983, 13; "University Workers Go on Strike", *Express*, 17 April 1980, 2.
17. "Strike in Mind", *Express*, 15 April 1980, 3.
18. Ibid.
19. Ibid.
20. "UWI Willing to Talk but Strike Must End First", *Trinidad Guardian*, 19 April 1980, 2.
21. "Strike in Mind", 3.
22. Ibid.
23. Ibid.
24. "Students Guild Taking Legal Action Against Cops", *Guardian*, 23 April 1980, 2.
25. "500 Students Oppose Fee Increases", *Students' Voice*, November 1982, 1.
26. Terri Ann Joseph, "The President's Report", *Undergrad*, 1 March 1984, 1.
27. Wayne Hayde, "A Changing Society", *Fusion*, October 1989, 14.
28. Ibid.
29. Editorial, *Embryo*, December 1982, 2.
30. "Be Aware: Elections Is Here", *Embryo*, 14 March 1983, 4.
31. Editorial, *Embryo*, 14 March 1983, 5.
32. "A Message from the Committee", *Fusion*, 1985, 2.
33. Ibid., 3.
34. "Road to Elections", *Undergrad*, November 1983, 2.
35. Editorial, *Embryo*, 14 March 1983, 2.
36. "ICC/Games Week", *Undergrad*, November 1983, 7.
37. "ICC Report", *Fusion*, October 1989, 14.
38. Philbert Williams, "Dear Editor", *FAGS Newsletter*, 1984, 3.
39. Wayne Hayde, "A Message from the President", *Fusion*, September 1987, 2.
40. "From the Guild", *Cote Ci Cote La*, 9 November 1987, 2.
41. "Guild Crisis", *Undergrad*, 17 November 1983, 11.
42. "On the 1980 Elections", *Indian Campus Review*, February 1980, 19.
43. "The Guild Elections Report 1985", *Fusion*, May 1985, 17.
44. Editorial, *Embryo*, 14 March 1983, 2.
45. Ibid.
46. "Roodal Moonilal", *Fusion*, September 1987, 7.
47. "International Students Day", *Undergrad*, 17 November 1983, 11.
48. "Arts Week", *Cote Ci Cote La*, November 1987, 1.
49. "UWI Teaching by Satellite Courses Beamed to No-Campus Islands", *On Campus Freshman's Guide, 1983–84* (St Augustine, Trinidad: The University of the West Indies, 1983), 1.
50. Minutes of meeting of the University Academic Committee, 11 December 1980 (UWIA, UWI St Augustine).

51. Ibid.
52. Minutes of meeting of the St Augustine Planning and Estimates Committee, 4 February 1981 (UWIA, UWI St Augustine).
53. Ibid.

Chapter 5

1. Guild council president Ansil Morris, correspondence to prime minister of Jamaica P.J. Patterson, 3 June 1993 (UWIA, UWI St Augustine).
2. Professor Compton Bourne, correspondence to guild president Marlon Jameson, 30 September 1996 (UWIA, UWI St Augustine). 56.
3. Patrick Gomez, letter to the editor, *Socialite*, October 1990, 6.
4. Clarence Rambharat, "Security: Not Just an Elections Issue", *Fusion*, October 1990, 25.
5. Students' Guild, *Report on Students' Guild Activities, 1991/1992* (St Augustine, Trinidad and Tobago: University of the West Indies, 1991), 1–2.
6. Students' Guild, *Report*, 1.
7. Ibid., 1.
8. "Report on the Campus Visit by Delegates to the International Symposium on Second Messenger Systems", *Fusion*, 1994, 24.
9. Students' Guild, *Guild Annual Report 1992–1993* (St Augustine, Trinidad and Tobago: University of the West Indies, 1992), 2.
10. Ibid.
11. "Simple Thoughts", *Socialite*, October 1990, 4.
12. "From 'A' Level Student to Undergrad: Impressions of an ex-Fresher" *Socialite*, October 1990, 16.
13. Dennis Brown, "The Enigma of Student Inaction", *Socialite*, October 1990, 8.
14. Ibid., 8.
15. "From the Editor", *Arts in Motion*, 1991, 1.
16. Ibid., 4.
17. "Viewpoint", *Arts in Motion*, 1991, 4–5.
18. "Guild Elections", *Arts in Motion*, 1991, 11.
19. Students' Guild, *Report*, 2.
20. Ibid., 2.
21. "A Nightmare Come True", *Fusion*, 1993, 6.
22. Ibid., 6.
23. Guild president Ansil Morris, correspondence to Professor Maxwell Richards, 26 July 1993 (UWIA, UWI St Augustine).
24. Ibid.

25. Sheldon Poujade, "President's Message", *Fusion*, 1990, 2.
26. Ibid.
27. Gerard Thomas, "The EAC Speaks", *Socialite*, October 1990, 9.
28. Ibid.
29. Anil Singh, "The Guild in Perspective", *Fusion*, October 1991, 24.
30. Ansil Morris, "A Word from the President", *Fusion*, September 1993, 4.
31. Ibid., 4.
32. Anil Singh, "The Guild in Perspective", *Fusion*, October 1991, 24.
33. Students' Guild, *Guild Annual Report*, 8.
34. Ibid., 4.
35. Guild vice-president Dionne Ligoure, correspondence to Principal Maxwell Richards, 28 October 1994 (UWIA, UWI St Augustine).
36. Guild council president Elton Wickham, correspondence to former president Ansil Morris, 28 March 1994 (UWIA, UWI St Augustine).
37. Guild students, correspondence to Professor Richards, 23 September 1994 (UWIA, UWI St Augustine).
38. Ligoure, correspondence to Richards.
39. "Letters to the Editor", *Socialite*, October 1990, 5.
40. Ibid.
41. "Official Statement of the UWI Islamic Society on the July 27th Events", *Muslim Students' Voice*, October 1990, 5.

Chapter 6

1. Attorney Devesh Maharaj, correspondence to UWI principal Bhoe Tewarie, 25 September 2001 (UWIA, UWI St Augustine).
2. Hong Ping, correspondence to Guild President Navindra Ramnanan, 18 September 2001 (UWIA, UWI St Augustine).
3. Devesh Maharaj, correspondence to the registrar of the Supreme Court, 17 May 2001 (UWIA, UWI St Augustine).
4. Ibid.
5. Minutes of meeting on the Guild president dispute, 24 October 2001 (UWIA, UWI St Augustine).
6. Randolph Hezekiah, correspondence to Navindra Ramnanan, 6 April 2001 (UWIA, UWI St Augustine).
7. Danny Maharaj, correspondence to Jacob Opadeyi, 17 April 2002 (UWIA, UWI St Augustine).
8. Denzil Mohammed, "Bacchanal Baton", *Trinidad Guardian*, 25 April 2003.
9. Kenrick Nobbee and Ann Marie Bissessar, correspondence to secretary of the Guild, 11 April 2003 (UWIA, UWI St Augustine).

10. Ibid.
11. Ibid.
12. Ibid
13. Indarjit Seuraj, "UWI Students Vote Today for New Guild", *Trinidad Guardian*, 14 April 2005.
14. Ibid.
15. Indarjit Seuraj, "UWI Election under Probe", *Trinidad Guardian*, 20 April, 2005.
16. Indarjit Seuraj, "New Guild Gets Green Light", *Trinidad Guardian*, 27 April 2005.
17. Bhoe Tewarie, "Let Us Fix what Needs Fixing", *STAN*, October 2003–March 2004.
18. "Connect with Dr Glenn Ramadhar-Singh", *STAN*, July–September 2004, 42.
19. Minutes of University Finance and General Purposes Committee, 7 February 2003 (UWIA, UWI St Augustine).
20. Akins Vidale, correspondence to campus registrar William Iton, 26 March 2004 (UWIA, UWI St Augustine).
21. Ibid.
22. Clint Fernandez, correspondence to campus registrar William Iton, 24 July 2004 (UWIA, UWI St Augustine).
23. David Moses, acting campus registrar, correspondence to Clint Fernandez, 28 July 2004 (UWIA, UWI St Augustine).
24. "Connect with Dr Glenn Ramadhar-Singh", 29.
25. Student Guild council, correspondence to members of campus council, 7 March 2006 (UWIA, UWI St Augustine).
26. "What's Going On", *Your Guild*, no. 3 (November 2005): 4.
27. *The Constitution of the Guild of Students* (St Augustine, Trinidad and Tobago: The University of the West Indies, 2009), iii.
28. Ibid.
29. "Season of the King", *STAN*, July–September 2002, 3.
30. Campus registrar, correspondence to Guild president Kajita Khan, 12 April 2000 (UWIA, UWI St Augustine).
31. Anthony Perry, correspondence to J. Jebodsingh, Thelora Reynolds and Victor Cowan, 31 October 2001 (UWIA, UWI St Augustine).
32. "Chancellor Talks With Students on Walk-about", *STAN*, July–September 2004.
33. Ibid.
34. "What's Going On", 5.
35. "Parking on Campus", *Your Guild*, no. 4 (December 2005): 14.
36. Ibid.
37. Miranda La Rose, "UWI Meetings, Classes Cancelled", *Trinidad Express*, 11 November 2010.
38. Ibid.
39. Denzil Mohammed, "Bacchanal Baton", 25 April 2003, *Trinidad Guardian*.

40. "Connect with Dr Glenn Ramadhar-Singh", 42.
41. Ibid.
42. "Fallon's Fate: Inside the New Guild of Students", *STAN*, July–September 2005, 23.
43. Professor Clement Sankat, "Safety at the Helm of Our Concern", *UWI Today*, February 2012.
44. Brennon Patterson, "UWI Carnival: A Privilege or a Right?" (letter to the editor), *Trinidad Express*, 5 February 2012.
45. "HIV/AIDS Awareness on Campus" *Your Guild*, no. 4 (December 2005): 5.
46. Ibid.
47. *UWI Annual Report 2007–2008* (St Augustine, Trinidad and Tobago: University of the West Indies, 2008), 25.
48. *UWI Annual Report 2008–2009* (St Augustine, Trinidad and Tobago: University of the West Indies, 2009), 19.
49. Ibid.
50. Kieran Khan, "A Message from Your PCC", *Your Guild*, no. 3, (November 2005): 3.
51. Minutes of University Finance and General Purposes Committee, 7 February 2003 (UWIA, UWI St Augustine).
52. Ibid.
53. Ibid.
54. *UWI Annual Report 2005–2006* (St Augustine, Trinidad and Tobago: University of the West Indies, 2006), 83.
55. LAB RAT #411, "UWI Students Treated Like Lab Rats", *Newsday*, 5 March 2004.
56. Denzil Mohammed, "Campus Politics", *Trinidad Guardian*, 2 April 2006.
57. Kenrick Nobbee, correspondence to Reshma Jagai, 9 April 2003 (UWIA, UWI St Augustine).
58. "What's Going On", *Your Guild*, no. 3 (November 2005): 4.
59. Sandra Singh, "UWI's Agents of Change", *Newsday*, 26 April 2008.
60. Ibid.
61. Sandra Sookram, Maukesh Basdeo, Kerry Sumesar-Rai and George Saridakis, "A Time-series Analysis of Crime in Trinidad and Tobago", Sir Arthur Lewis Institute of Social and Economic Working Paper no. 20 (St Augustine, Trinidad and Tobago: University of the West Indies, 2009).
62. Ibid.
63. Ibid.
64. "Parking on Campus" *Your Guild* no. 4 (December 2005): 14.
65. "Fallon's Fate", *STAN*, July–September 2005, 23.
66. Ibid.
67. Clint Chan Tack, "UWI Elections in Limbo", *Newsday*, 10 April 2008.

Selected Bibliography

The following collection of sources are some of the documentation used to craft the narrative, in addition to correspondence housed in the University of the West Indies Archives.

Publications by the Guild of Students

Embryo
Guild Annual Report
Guild Bulletin
Insight
Magnet
Augustinian
Your Guild

Publications by Student Clubs and Societies

Arts in Motion
Cote Ci Cote La
FAGS
Fresher's Guide
Freshman's Guide
Fusion
Indian Campus Review
Opinion
Riteflow
Canadian
Muslim Students' Voice
Undergrad

Socialite
Students for Change
Students' Voice

PUBLICATIONS PRODUCED BY THE UWI

On Campus Freshman's Guide
Pelican Annual
Sundowner
STAN
University of the West Indies Annual Report

NEWSPAPERS

Newsday
Trinidad Guardian
Express
Vanguard

Secondary Sources

Armitage A.L., J.Z. Bowers, C. Iverson, H. Leussink. *West Indies: Development of the University of the West Indies, May–June 1968*. Paris: UNESCO, 1968.

Brereton, Bridget. *From Imperial College to University of the West Indies: A History of the St Augustine Campus, Trinidad and Tobago*. Kingston: Ian Randle, 2011.

Hall, Douglas. *The University of the West Indies: A Quinquagenary Calendar, 1948–1998*. Kingston: The Press, University of the West Indies, 1998.

Lawrence, Vernon L. "A Look at UWI". In *The Voice of the Hermits*. St Augustine, Trinidad and Tobago: The University of the West Indies, 1976.

Rétout, Marie Thérèse. *A Light Rising from the West*. Port of Spain: Inprint Caribbean, 1985.

Ryan Selwyn, Taimoon Stewart and Roy McCree, eds. *The Black Power Revolution 1970: A Retrospective*. St Augustine, Trinidad and Tobago: Institute of Social and Economic Research, University of the West Indies, 1995.

Sookram, Sandra, Maukesh Basdeo, Kerry Sumesar-Rai and George Saridakis, "A Time-series Analysis of Crime in Trinidad and Tobago", Sir Arthur Lewis Institute of Social and Economic Working Paper no. 20 (St Augustine, Trinidad and Tobago: University of the West Indies, 2009). http://sta.uwi.edu/salises/pubs/workingpapers/ATimeSeriesAnalysisOfCrimeTrinidadandTobago.pdf.

Students' Guild. *Report on Students' Guild Activities, 1991/1992*. St Augustine, Trinidad: The University of the West Indies. 1991.

———. *Guild Annual Report 1992–1993*. St Augustine, Trinidad: The University of the West Indies. 1992.

Student Guild Council. *The Constitution of the Guild of Students*. St Augustine, Trinidad and Tobago: University of the West Indies, 2009.

Index

Academic Committee, 60, 61
academic staff, xii, 81–82
administration, St Augustine, xii–xiii
    relationship with Guild, 18, 21, 23–24, 37, 81
    student perceptions of, xiii, 3, 43
Advisory Committee on Sport, 44
African Caribbean identity, development of, 26–27, 28, 39, 50–51
Alcohol Use Disorder survey, 85
Alexander, Michael, 75
Alleyne, Sir George, 80–81
Als, Michael, 27
Alumni Association, St Augustine, xii
Andalcio, Russell, 29
Annual Festival of Arts, Craft, and Literature, 41–42
anti-colonialist movements, 27, 41
Antigua, 14
Appointment (Placements) Board, 44
Archer, Victor, 11, 12
Art Group (ICTA), 2
Arts Annual, 32–33
Arts in Motion, 66, 67
Arts Week, 59
Association Football Club (ICTA), 2
Augustinian, 3, 8, 9

Baker, Mobafa, 77, 80, 86
Barnes, Dr Junor, 65

Bartolo, Ronald Lindsay, 5
Beddoe, Peter, 58
Belgrave, Ian, 45–46
Bert Bailey and the Jets, 17
Best, Lloyd, 20
binge drinking, 85
Birdsong, 36, 45–46
Black Power movement, xiii, 24, 26–27, 32, 42
Blackwood, Carl, 26, 29, 91
Board for Examinations, 52
bookshop, 17
Bookshop Committee, 44
Bourne, Compton, 63
Bowen, F.H., 10–11
"Brain Drain", 28
Braithwaite, Lloyd, 39, 43, 53, 60
Brereton, Bridget, 2, 13, 26, 38, 39
Brewster, Vernon, 45
British West Indies federation, 13
Brooks, Oliver Stanley, 5, 11
Brown, Dennis, 59, 67
Building and Grounds Committee, 44
Burgess, Reginald Alfred, 5
Burke, Maurice, 76, 79
Burroughs, Randolph, 53
Burt, Arthur E., 12

Cafeteria Committee, 44
CAHIERS complaint system, 81

Campus Academic Board, 34, 44, 52
Campus Carnival, 17, 45, 83–84, 92
Campus Council, 52
Campus Examinations Committees, 44
campus security, 64, 70, 81, 88–89
Canada Hall, 7, 9, 51, 53, 55, 64
Canadian, 7–8, 9, 25–26, 31, 32
Caribbean Community (CARICOM) Heads of Government meeting, 63
Caribbean Federation of Youth Congress, 86
Caribbean Inter-Collegiate Debating Competition, 62–63, 92
"Caribbean Leadership in Training", 65
Caribbean Reasonings lectures, 85, 92
Caribbean Union of Tertiary Students, 59
Carmichael, Stokely, 26, 27
Carnegie, A.R., 35
Caroni, march to, 24
Cenac, Kelvin, 79
Chalmers, W.S., 44
Chang, Carlisle, 22
Chesney, Hilbertus A.D., 4
Civil Rights movement (U.S.), 26
Clarke, Austin, 12
College of Arts and Science, St Augustine, 12
Committee on Tuition Fees, 68
committees, student representation on, 43–44, 51–52
community outreach, 36
Conference of Black Writers (Montreal), 21
Conferences on East Indians, 38
Congress of Black Writers (Montreal), 27
Constitution Committee, 79
Constitution Drafting Committee, 60

constitutional reform, xiv, 1, 2–3, 10–12, 33–35, 60–61, 77–79, 92
Cote Ci Cote La, 54, 55
Cowan, Victor, 62–63
crime, 88–89
Cuban Revolution, 26
cultural heritage, consciousness of, xiii, 26–27, 28, 38–39
Culture Club (ICTA), 2
Cumberbatch, Casey, 85

Daaga, Makandal. *See* Granger, Geddes
Daaga Auditorium, xiv
Daaga Hall, 24, 43
dances, 3
D'Arbeau, Dave (Khafra Kambon), 24, 28, 29
Debating Society, 62–63
Decentralization, Committee on, 44
DeGannes, Dominique Norman Percival (Percy), 4, 5, 10–11
Distance Teaching Experiment system, 59–60, 92
Dominica, 14, 32
Douglas, Sean, 58

Edwards, Harry, 27
Elder, J.D., 45
Elections Committee, 76
"Elections in Perspective", *Embryo*, 40
Embryo, 30–31, 32, 39–41, 42, 52–53, 54–55, 58
enrolment levels, 2, 3, 12–13, 20, 95–96
ethnic conflicts, xiii, 48–50, 51
ethnic identity, and socio-economic class, 20
Evolution Series conference, 63–64
Express, 29, 84

External Affairs Commission (EAC), 13–14
Extra Mural Advisory Committee, 44
extra-curricular activities, 3, 36, 66–67

Faculty of Agriculture, St Augustine, 2, 5, 13
Faculty of Arts and General Studies, 66
Faculty of Arts and General Studies Newsletter, 55
Faculty of Arts and Science, 22
Faculty of Engineering, St Augustine, 2, 5, 13, 38
Faculty of Liberal Arts, 5
Faculty of Social Sciences Guild, 66
Fanon, Frantz, *Dying Colonialism*, 31
Fernandes, Noel Ivor, 5
Fernandez, Clint, 78–79
Finance and General Purposes Committee, 52, 60, 78, 87
Finance Assessment Committee, 60–61
Finance Committee, 44
Flying Squad (police), 53
Forman, James, 27
Fraser, Eric L., 12
Free Trade Area of the Americas, 87
Fresher's Guide (later as *Freshman's Guide*), 4, 17
Freshman's Ball, 17
Freshman's Guide, 46
Fusion, 49, 55, 56, 58, 64, 66, 69, 70

Gannessingh, Winston Krishna, 31
Ghany, Dr Hamid, 63
Gibson, Hugh, 33, 34, 35, 44
Gilly, Adolfo, 31
Golf Club (ICTA), 2
Gonzales, Anthony, 14
Gonzalves, Maurice, 31
Granger, Geddes, xiii, 21–22, 29, 91
    as council president, 20, 22–26, 30, 33
Grant, Marlon, 85
Gregoire, Sheridan, 33
Grenada, 4, 5, 14, 59
Grenadian Students' Association, 59
Grenadines Students Association, 87
Grimes, Natasha, 89
"grubs"/"grub week", 17, 46, 51, 56
Guardian, 29, 31, 50, 53
Guild Bulletin, 9
Guild council, Cave Hill
    code of ethics, 78, 92
    Inter-Campus Guild council, 86–87, 92
    leadership training initiative, 80
    regional Guild meetings, 59–60, 65
Guild council, Mona
    code of ethics, 78, 92
    Inter-Campus Guild council, 86–87, 92
    leadership training initiative, 80
    regional Guild meetings, 59–60, 65
Guild council, St Augustine, xii, 4–5, 14, 17, 48, 86–87
    academic standards of councillors, 77
    accountability of, 54–55, 57–58
    centralization of UWI Guilds, 11–12
    code of ethics, 78, 92
    constitutional reform, 10–12, 33–35, 60–61, 77–79
    corruption and fraud allegations, 58, 77, 83
    election irregularities, 19–20, 49, 58, 67–68, 71–72, 74–77
    elections, and voter turnout, 67–68, 83, 88

Guild Council, St Augustine (*continued*)
   institutional development, 70
   Inter-Campus Guild council, 86–87, 92
   leadership training initiative, 80
   mass resignation of, 57, 92
   and party politics, 58–59, 89
   power of recall, 33, 34, 35, 75
   radicalism, 20–21, 28–30
   regional and international links, 13–14, 59–60, 64–65
   relationship with administration, xii, xiii, 18, 21, 23–24, 81
   student activities, xiii, 17, 35–36, 45–46, 56–57, 62–66
   student perceptions of, 69–70, 82–83
   suspension of president, 74–75, 92
Guild Hall, 4, 17, 23, 24
Guild of Graduates (UCWI), 2
Guild of Students, St Augustine, xiv, xii, 1
   club memberships, 61
   and international scholars, 65
   past presidents, 93–94
   perceptions of administration, xiii, 3
   regional and international links, 13–14, 59–60, 64–65
   strike by non-academic workers, 42–43, 52–53
   and student activities, xiii, 17, 35–36
   student/administration relationship, xiii, 3, 18, 21, 23–24, 37
Guild of Undergraduates, Mona, 2, 10–12
Guild of Undergraduates, St Augustine. *See* Guild of Students, St Augustine
Guyana, 5

Hall, Douglas, 43
Hall students, conflict with Trinidadian students, 51

Halls of Residence Committee, 44
Harris, E. Nigel, 81
Harvard Model United Nations debate, 87
Harvey, Franklyn Valantine Peter, 5, 11
Hayde, Wayne, 49, 56
Hemispherical Student Summit of the Americas, 87, 92
Hill, Robert, 27
HIV/AIDS, 84
Hockey Club (ICTA), 2
Holman, Ray, 45
Hoo, Kenneth George, 5
Huggins, Dudley, 23–24, 36
Hugh Wooding Law School, 83–84
Hurricane Tomas, 87

"I" room, 50, 55
ICC week, 35
Imperial College of Tropical Agriculture (ICTA), 2, 91
Indian Campus Review, 49, 55, 58
Indian community, 31, 38, 49–50
Indoor Games Club (ICTA), 2
Insight, 31, 32
Inter-Campus Committee (ICC), ICC week, 35
Inter-Campus Games, 45
Inter-Campus Guild council, 86–87, 92
Inter-Clubs Committee, 70
International Festival of Youth and Students (Venezuela), 87
International Student Conference, 14
International Symposium on Second Messenger Systems, 65
International Union of Students (IUS), Congress of, 65, 92
International Youth Day, 59, 64
Islamic Society (UWI), 72–73

Island People, 85
Iton, William, 78

Jackman, Anthony, 77
Jackman, Carl E., 12
Jamaat al Muslimeen insurrection, xiii, 72
Jamaica, 5
Jamaican Union of Tertiary Students, 65
James, Calvin, 63
James, C.L.R., 20, 22, 27
Jha, J.C., 31
John Donaldson Technical Institute, 84
Joint Consultative Committee, 44
Joseph, Terri-Ann, 57–58

kaiso music, 41–42
Kambon, Khafra (Dave D'Arbeau), 24, 28, 29
Karolinska Institute (Sweden), 65
Kenya, 87
Khan, Katija, 75, 80
Khan, Kieran, 86
King, Delf O., 11–12
King, Martin Luther, Jr, 26
Knott, Chevon, 79

leadership training initiative, 80
Lee-Own, Desmond Arthur, 5
Library Committee, 44
Ligoure, Dionne, 71–72
Lotus, 38
Lowhar, Syl, 24
Lutchmansingh, Fallon, 77, 79, 89

Magnet, 7, 9, 15–16, 17, 19, 31–32
Maharaj, Candace, 79
Maharaj, Danny, 75–76, 77

Maharaj, Devesh, 75
Management Studies, Department of, 61
Marshall, Bertie, 45
Martin, Godfrey, 44
Maynard, George Winston Cole, 5
McBurnie, Beryl, 22
Michener, Roland, 25, 91
Millette, James, 20
Mitchell, Krystal, 79
Mitchell, Roy, 21, 22
Mohammed, Denzil, 82–83, 88
Moonilal, Roodal, 59
Moore, Richard B., 27
Morean, Hillan, xiv, 79, 82, 88
Morris, Ansil, 63, 64, 68, 69–70, 71
Moses, David, 79
multinational corporations, and economic development, 20, 27
Murray, David (Aiyegoro Ome), 23, 24
Muslim Students' Voice, 72–73

Naipaul, Vidia, 22
Nathu, Jason, 86
National Affairs Committee, panel discussion, 63
National Alliance for Reconstruction, 59
National Debating Competition (UWI), 62–63, 92
National Joint Action Committee, 29
national politics, affiliations with Guild of Students, 58-59, 89
Natural History Society (ICTA), 2
Niles, Keron, 83
non-academic workers, xii–xiii
   strikes by, 42–43, 52–53, 91–92

Office of the Board of Undergraduate Studies, 80

Omatunde, Yusuf, 31
Ome, Aiyegoro, 23
Ome, Aiyegoro (David Murray), 24
Opadeyi, Jacob, 76
Open Lecture Series, 7
Open Lectures Committee, 44
Open University (UK), 65
Opinion, 9
Orientation Week events, 17, 46, 51, 56

Pan Trinbago, 45
Panday, Basdeo, 63
parking issues, 81
Parmasad, Kenneth, 31
"Party and Events Planning" lecture, 85
Patterson, P.J., 63
Pegasus movement, 22
Pelican, 23
People's National Movement (PNM), 48, 58–59, 63
Phillips, Wilfred, 7, 17
Pierre, Lennox, 45
Pilgrim, Alake, 83
Placement Board, 44
Planning and Estimate Committee, 44, 52, 61
Planters for Social Change, 84
poetry, in publications, 9, 10, 16
political activism, 20
  literary radicalism vs physical activism, 39–42
  Rodney travel prohibition, 21, 24, 25, 28
  Sir George Williams University incident, 25, 27, 29
  and student apathy, 7–8
  on student facilities and services, 52, 53
  student protests and demonstrations, 28–30, 37, 42–43, 52–53, 59, 81–82
  youth activism, 27
political expression, 55
  on attempted coup d'État, 72–73
  radicalization of publications, 30–33
  through humour and satire, 15–16
Port of Spain, march to, 26, 28, 91
Postgraduate Association, 81
power of recall, 33, 34, 35, 75
Prendergrast, Donisha, 85
public lectures, 7, 85
publications, St Augustine campus, 8–10, 15–16, 65–66
  Arts Annual, 32–33
  Arts in Motion, 66, 67
  Augustinian, 3, 8, 9
  Canadian, 7–8, 9, 25–26, 31, 32
  Cote Ci Cote La, 54, 55
  decline in, 85–86
  Embryo, 30–31, 32, 39–41, 42, 54–55, 58
  Express, 29, 84
  Faculty of Arts and General Studies Newsletter, 55
  freedom of expression, 55
  Fresher's Guide, 4
  Freshman's Guide, 46
  Fusion, 49, 55, 56, 58, 64, 66, 69, 70
  Guardian, 29, 50, 53
  Guild Bulletin, 9
  Indian Campus Review, 49–50, 55, 58
  Insight, 31, 32
  literary radicalism vs physical activism, 30–33, 39–42
  Lotus, 38
  Magnet, 7, 9, 19, 31–32
  Muslim Students' Voice, 72–73

Opinion, 9
Pelican, 23
Riteflow, 41–42, 50, 55
Socialite, 64, 66–67, 69, 72
St Augustine News (STAN), 85–86
Students for Change Manifesto, 41
Students' Voice, 55
Sundowner, 3, 6–7, 8–9, 15
"The Reporter", 66
Undergrad, 51, 52, 55, 56
Vanguard, 24, 28
The Voice of the Hermits, 41
Your Guild, 79, 83, 86, 89

race, and class relationships
   in Caribbean society, 24
   ethnic conflicts, 48–50, 51
   and student consciousness, 28–30, 38
racial discrimination, 7, 15, 24, 63
radicalism. *See* political activism
Ramadharsingh, Glenn, 77, 79, 83, 89
Rambachan, Surujrattan, 31
Rambharath, K. Clarence, 64, 72
Ramnanan, Navindra, 74–75, 92
Ramrekersingh, Augustus, 24
Ramtahal, Rejeanne, 67
Rastafari movement, 85
Ratiram, Ravi, 76, 77, 89
regional and international links, 13–14, 59–60, 64–65, 86–87
regional students, as on-campus residents, 4
Reid, Shaun A., 79
"The Reporter", 66
Richards, George Maxwell, 51
Rifle Shooting Club (ICTA), 2
Riteflow, 41–42, 50, 55
Riviere, Bill, 32

Roberts, Hugh, 64
Robertson, Dennis George, 5
Robinson, A.N.R., 29
Rodney, Walter, 9, 20, 27, 91
   travel prohibition, 21, 24, 25, 28
Rohlehr, Gordon, 45
Ross, Carlyle Bonstan Albert, 5
Rugby Football Club (ICTA), 2
Ryan, Selwyn, 50

Samaroo, Brinsley, 31
Sanatan, Amilcar, 85
Sankat, Clement, 82
Sealy, E. Henry, 14
Senate, 52
senior administrators, xiii
Sharma, Shiva, 54
Simon, Spree, 45
Sinanan, Khadija, 79
Singh, Anil, 70
Sir George Williams University incident, 25, 27, 29, 91
Smart, Winston, 29
social awareness, growth of, 28–30, 38
Socialite, 64, 66–67, 69, 72
Society for the Promotion of African Culture, 49
Society for the Propagation of Indian Culture (SPIC), 31, 49–50
socio-economic class, and ethnic identity, 20
South Africa, apartheid and, 59
SPIC (Society for the Propagation of Indian Culture), 31, 38, 49–50
sporting activities, 45
St Augustine News (STAN), 85–86
St Lucia, 14
St Lucian Students Association, 87

St Mary's College, 22, 35
St Vincent, 14
St Vincent Students Association, 87
Steelband Club, 45
Student Activity Centre, xiv
Student Advisory Services, 45, 62
Student Affairs Committee, 44
student apathy, 56, 66–68. *See also* political activism
   and extra-curricular activities, 3, 56
   reasons for, 67
   and social obligations, 6–8
   voter turnout, council elections, 67–68, 83, 88
student consciousness, and social awareness, 28–30, 38, 57, 62
student demographics, 13, 20, 39
student loans, 17
student parties, 64
Student Services, 46
student/administration relationship, xiii, 3, 18, 21, 37, 80–82
   fee increases, 53–54, 68–69, 80
   lunchtime series, 69
   student representation on committees, 43–44, 51–52
Students for Change Manifesto, 41–42
Students' Senate, disbanding of, 78
Student's Society, 10
Students Today Alumni Tomorrow (UWI), 79
Students' Voice, 55
Summit of the Americas, 87
Sundowner, 3, 6–7, 8–9, 15
Suttie, J.M., 2
Swimming Pool Committee, 44

"teach-ins", 7

Tennis Club (ICTA), 2
Tewarie, Dr Bhoe, 77
Thomas, Clive Y., 28
Trinidad and Tobago, 5, 29
   attempted coup d'état, 72–73
   crime, 88–89
   foreign ownership of resources, 20, 27
   government funding of university, 38
   High Court injunctions against Guild council, 75, 77
   as industrial nation, 37–38
   People's National Movement (PNM), 48, 58–59
Trinidad and Tobago Students' Movement, 53
Trinidad Express, 82
Trinidad Guardian, 82
Triniscene, 85
Trinity Hall food park, 84

Undergrad, 51, 52, 55, 56
United National Congress, 63, 89
United Nations Geoguthic Movement, 63
United States. *See also* Black Power movement
   Civil Rights movement, 26
   and Latin American scholarships, 14
"Unity, Imperialism, and Cricket", *Embryo*, 40
Unity March against racism, 63
University and Allied Workers' Union strike, 52–53
University College of West Indies (UCWI), 1–3, 91
University Council, 52
University of London (UK), 1–2
University of Saskatchewan (Canada), 65

University of the West Indies,
    Bridgetown, 11–12
University of the West Indies, Cave Hill
    fee increases, 68–69
    and Guild constitution, 35
    Inter-Campus Games, 45
    student activism, 24
University of the West Indies, Mona
    centralization of UWI Guilds, 10–12
    fee increases, 68–69
    strike by non-academic workers, 42
    student activism, 24
University of the West Indies, St Augustine, 2, 12–13, 31, 91–92. *See also* administration, St Augustine
    as commuter campus, 68
    enrolment levels, 2, 3, 12–13, 20, 95–96
    faculties. *See specific faculties by name*
    fee increases, 53–54, 68–69, 80
    government funding of, 38
    placement services, 39
    student demographics, 13, 20, 39
University of the West Indies (UWI)
    establishment of, 1–2

Vanguard, 24, 28
Vidale, Akins, 78
The Voice of the Hermits, 41

Wallace, Wendell, 86
Warner, Francis, 60
Wellington, Karl, 5
West Indies Group of University Teachers (WIGUT), 53, 81–82
Wickham, Elton, 71–72
Williams, A., 11
Williams, Eric, 13, 15, 24, 25, 38
"A Wonderful Journey", *Indian Campus Review*, 50
Woodstock committee, 31
World Universities Debating Championship, 63

X, Malcolm, 26

Yale University choir, 35
Younge, Weygand Fitz David, 5
Your Guild, 79, 83, 86, 89
youth activism, 27

Zen Buddhism lecture, 85

www.ingramcontent.com/pod-product-compliance
Lightning Source LLC
Chambersburg PA
CBHW020856160426
43192CB00007B/948